CONFESSING THE FAITH

CONFESSING THE FAITH

**REFORMERS DEFINE
THE CHURCH, 1530–1580**

Robert Kolb

CONCORDIA PUBLISHING HOUSE · SAINT LOUIS

Copyright © 1991 Concordia Publishing House
3558 S. Jefferson Avenue, St. Louis, MO 63118-3968
Manufactured in the United States of America

Library of Congress Cataloging-in-Publication Data

Kolb, Robert, 1941–
    Confessing the faith : reformers define the Church, 1530–1580 /
  Robert A. Kolb.
        p. cm. — (Concordia scholarship today)
        Includes bibliographical references.
        ISBN 0-570-04556-8
        1. Lutheran Church—Creeds—History and criticism. 2. Lutheran Church—
Catechisms—History and criticism. 3. Lutheran Church—Germany—History—16th
century. 4. Reformation—Germany. 5. Germany—Church history—16th century.
I. Title. II. Series.
BX8068.A1K65   1991
238'.41'09031—dc20   90-27311

5 6 7 8 9 10 11   07 06 05 04 03

Contents

Foreword

Confessing the Faith offers historical insights that relate to current concerns. The book assumes that a broadened and deepened understanding of the historical setting of the proclamation of the Lutheran faith will clarify and enrich our analysis of issues that beset us today and in so doing help us to "comprehend the love of Christ."

According to God's Word, Christians are theological and must think theologically about all matters of life. There is no such thing as a nondenominational view of God's Word. Any Christian who confesses Christ immediately begins the journey into the history of Christ and His deeds on earth. The journey begins in the Old and New Testaments and continues now in the life of the church that confesses what Christ gave to her in the Holy Scriptures. For this reason, every confession of Christ is another step in the history of Christ on earth as He comes to us through His Word and Sacraments. This sacramental life is the history of Christ as He acts to forgive sin through His bride, the church.

This book studies the past to better understand the present march of the history of the church. It describes how Lutherans of the 16th century produced the documents that came to be known collectively as the Lutheran Confessions, which were eventually united in *The Book of Concord* in 1580. These documents are their confession to the world how Christ's person, work, and gifts of Word and Sacraments define particular positions as either standing in harmony with Him and His church or standing against Him in sinful rebellion. But does confessionalism remain relevant today? Do we want or need systematized statements of biblical doctrine in a democratic nation that cultivates and commends individualism, protects the right of privacy, and eagerly assimilates people of other faiths who come to the United States?

Some Christian denominations have not emphasized creedal statements to the extent Lutherans do. A few have no formal statements of faith at all, relying for their religious base on a community of spirit or the momentary view of a given denominational leader. Lutherans, however, stand with the overwhelming majority of those who adhere to historical Christianity and fully understand that Christ taught His church to confess His truth. Therefore, the Lutheran Confessions are no more and no less than the reflection or sum of what the Scriptures proclaim.

Lutherans firmly contend that all Christians are members of the body of Christ, and they strongly support true ecumenical endeavors. Lutherans believe that the true church is one and unique and that she hears her Lord. What the church hears from the Word of the Lord is what is confessed; therein lies the basis of true ecumenical work. For Lutherans, a clear understanding of biblical doctrine, as summarized in the Lutheran Confessions, is helpful in conversation with fellow Christians. Such a conversation can and ought to lead to a common understanding of Christian teaching. With such a perspective, Lutherans can enthusiastically engage in theological dialogue, respectful of the other persons involved while in all humility and servitude still confessing and proclaiming the truth of the faith as described in the Lutheran Confessions.

The social climate of the 21st century is hungry for stability, congruence, and truth. The latter part of the 20th century introduced the extreme relativism of postmodern thinking. At the same time, our climate has little patience for a belligerent and arrogant approach to confessing the faith. Sometimes texts from the 16th century sound confrontational and inappropriate to the 21st-century ear. However, as one mines the substance of these confessions, one grasps why such strident language is evident as one confesses the faith in humility but from the position of confidence in and certainty of salvation through the work of Jesus. It is the publisher's hope that this book will bring to light the overwhelming parallels between the need to confess Christ exhibited in the 16th and the 21st centuries.

Rev. Mark E. Sell
Senior Editor—Academic and Professional Books
Concordia Publishing House

Preface

For four and a half centuries, growing up in a Lutheran family has usually meant, among other things, being taught to confess. Lutheran boys and girls learn early on to confess certain key passages of the Bible and the ancient creeds of the church. Like millions of other Lutheran parents, my parents began to acquaint me with the Small Catechism long before I had any idea what a "confessional writing" might be. Indeed, I remember when a counselor at a youth camp, with a gleam in his eyes and excitement in his voice, told us about his recent reading of the Formula of Concord, a document I had not yet heard of.

My knowledge of the Lutheran Confessions grew in seminary and in my doctoral studies with several professors, including Ralph Bohlmann, Arthur Carl Piepkorn, Robert Preus, Carl S. Meyer, and Robert Kingdon. They inspired me to delve more deeply into the world of the 16th-century Lutheran confessors. Students in my classroom and fellow members of congregations have led me more deeply into the Gospel those confessors believed and taught. The fruits of a quarter-century of study of the Lutheran Confessions appear in this book.

Confessing the faith is simply a part of following Christ and a vital part of the Christian life. It has taken on particular significance in the Lutheran church because of the way in which Lutherans conceive of their calling as believers, and because of the historic circumstances in which our confessions were born. In this volume, I explore the implications of the fact that Lutherans have always viewed themselves as "confessional"—and thus "confessing."

My account is largely historical, but the history of one's own church has great practical significance. The bold confessions of our 16th-century forefathers serve as a model and an inspiration for all contemporary Christians who likewise want to proclaim the saving Gospel of Jesus Christ to the world. The confessors at Augsburg delivered an evangelical confession because it was centered in the Gospel of Jesus Christ. Their confession was evangelistic, for they were committed to proclaim Christ's name to peoples far and wide. They tried to do this through the translation and publication of their confessions throughout Christendom. Their confession was ecumenical, for they believed that it represented the faith of the one, holy, catholic, and apostolic church. They confessed in order to call all Christians back to the Gospel that Christ had given to His church. Their confession was eschatological, for they were acutely aware that on judgment day they would stand before the throne of the God whom they were confessing. They were also aware that their confession possessed an eschatological urgency for a humanity which had strayed from its Creator.

This volume is not the product of the author alone. Without the support of the library staffs at the Herzog August Bibliothek in Wolfenbüttel, Federal Republic of Germany; Luther Northwestern Theological Seminary, Saint Paul, Minnesota; Concordia Seminary, Saint Louis, Missouri; and the Center for Reformation Research, Saint Louis, Missouri, it would not have been possible to do the research for this study. Five friends—two pastors and three professors—reviewed the text and aided me greatly in refining it. They are Vernon Gundermann, John Pless, James Kittelson, James Nestingen, and Oliver Olson. Wilbert Rosin and the staff at Concordia Publishing House have helped much by shepherding the manuscript through the editorial process. Robert V. Schnucker, managing editor of *The Sixteenth Century Journal,* gave permission to revise substantially an article which appeared in that journal, "German Lutheran Interpretations of the Diet of Augsburg to 1577," and to publish these revisions as Chapter Two of this book. My wife, Pauline, again gave me invaluable research assistance, offered warm support and critical reaction, and, with our daughter Kelley, lent time to complete the writing. To all I am deeply grateful.

Robert Kolb

Concordia College, Saint Paul
June 25, 1990,
the 460th Anniversary of the Presentation
of the Augsburg Confession

Abbreviations

LW   Luther's Works. American Edition. 55 vols. Jaroslav Pelikan and Helmut T. Lehmann, general editors. St. Louis: Concordia; Philadelphia: Fortress, 1955–86.

WA   *D. Martin Luthers Werke. Kritische Gesamtausgabe.* Weimar: Böhlau, 1883–.

1

Confessing Christ from Augsburg to the Nations

The Apostle Paul stood before the Roman governors Felix and Festus and before King Agrippa. As he did so, he confessed his faith (Acts 24–26). Paul may have had in mind the example of Christ Himself, who confessed who He was before the high priest Caiaphas (Matt. 26:62–68). When the early Christians refused to take the Roman empire's pledge of allegiance, which included worship of the emperor, they confessed their faith and followed the examples of Christ and Paul. Often they testified to their faith by giving their life, and thus they earned the title "martyr." Paul himself argued that Christians naturally confess their faith, for the confession of faith flows from the lips of those who are saved (Rom. 10:10). From a Biblical perspective words are vital, in the deepest sense of that word. For certain words are God's instruments to give and sustain life. God spoke the universe into existence (Gen. 1:3, 6, 9, 11, 14, 24) and came into human flesh as the Word (John 1:1–18), and God's power lies in the word of the Gospel (Rom. 1:16). God's people too must speak that word of the Gospel. Throughout Christian history, they always have.

Although Christians had been confessing their faith for centuries, there was something unique about the 16th-century confession of faith delivered in the south German city of Augsburg in the year 1530, an event that changed the way in which Western Christians think about themselves today. Late in the spring of 1530 the eyes of the Holy Roman Empire were riveted on Augsburg, where the emperor, Charles V, was coming to conduct the affairs of his German empire at a diet (the meeting of the empire's legislature). The invading armies of the Ottoman Turks still cast a long, dark shadow across western Europe even though they had been hurled back from the gates of Vienna the previous autumn. And so the Turkish threat to western civilization would command the attention of the princes and representatives of towns as they gathered to deliberate with Charles V. This diet still attracts attention today, however, and not because of its response to the Turkish menace, but because at Augsburg in 1530, seven princes of the empire and the representatives of two imperial cities stood before the emperor—in effect, before the entire empire—to confess their faith. Since then, their words have defined the faith confessed by millions of people in many parts of the world.

From Confession to Church

Suddenly the Lutheran church was there, though those who witnessed its birth only later realized that the imperial diet had played midwife to the birth of a new *confession* and therefore a new church. This new ecclesiastical body was the first of several that emerged from the 16th-century reorganization of Western Christendom. Hermann Sasse labeled the church of the Augsburg Confession "the confessional church *par excellence.*" It suddenly emerged, not as an organization, and yet as a church. It had no form of government, nor episcopal or synodical organs to represent it. So the imperial estates represented it before the political world, and a few theologians—led by Philip Melanchthon—before the ecclesiastical world. It had no legal existence, but it did have its basic teaching, the Confession.[1]

That lay people confessed their faith before Emperor Charles V at Augsburg was not unique. Such lay confessions had taken place countless times in the history of the church. Nor was it unusual that their confession took place in the national spotlight, in Augsburg, the economic heart of Germany at that time and the focus of political attention during the diet. Christians often confessed their faith in the meeting halls and on the streets of the city. But this confession was different. Though a few documents as old or older do continue to command the attention of modern scholars, few documents from the Middle Ages have been scrutinized so intensely and debated even in recent years such as this confession at Augsburg.[2]

Never before, however, had a confession of faith delivered in a public forum by lay people acquired ecclesiastical or theological authority. Not since the Council of Nicea had a confession created

14

in such a forum become a standard of dogma, a secondary authority for teaching the faith, and a key in the interpretation of Scripture. Not since Nicea had such a confession become a fundamental definition of what Christians believe and teach. The document immediately set the standard by which the Augsburg confessors themselves and their followers were to be judged; and it became their agenda as they proclaimed, taught, and lived out the Christian life.

This confession defined the essence of the church of Christ. Werner Elert observed that "With [the Augsburg Confession] began a fresh assumption of form by the Christian church. The binding together of the many in a community of hearing is form. The chorale is form. The confession is form. Proclamation itself is form. Each of these is a shaping of the many into a unity."[3]

At Augsburg, the Lutheran princes and cities could have achieved a common expression of their faith, and thus unity, in any of three ways. Philip of Hesse proposed an ecclesiastical defense league of Lutheran princes. Another alternative was a binding constitution for the various churches that would have obligated them to follow certain standards of practice as well as to bind themselves in unity of teaching. Instead, the Lutheran confessors chose a third alternative. They limited their unity to a united confession of the faith.[4] Their *act* of confessing the faith and the resulting confessional charter changed the meaning of *confession* for much of Christendom. The act of confessing the faith epitomizes the nature of the Lutheran movement and its churches.

The Nature of Christian Confession

Understanding the story of the Augsburg Confession calls for an excursus on *confession*. "To be human is to confess," Arthur C. Cochrane has commented.[5] The natural course of human life leads every individual and institution to point publicly to its core of beliefs and values in one way or another. Yet some religions do not move their adherents to make public confession. Particularly in a society that values individual freedom of belief and that considers beliefs to be relative rather than absolute, a verbal confession of one's beliefs is not natural, because confession of what is true includes, at least by implication, rejecting what is false. Confessing the faith

15

requires rejection of everything that contradicts and threatens the faith. Therefore, although one might expect otherwise, confession does not mark the lives of the adherents of every religion or system of belief and value. Nevertheless, the God who has spoken to His people in Scripture and has called His church into being through prophetic and apostolic voices still calls His church likewise to speak and confess its faith.

A confession of faith may be defined as "a formal, usually (though not always) brief, summary of the central principles of a religion, fixed in its wording. Alongside the task of comprehending the essential content of a faith, it has the function of demarcating that faith in relationship to other religions and heretical tendencies within its own adherents."[6] This definition can be expanded to include not only the functions of self-definition and demarcation but also those of establishing and preserving the community of faith, of proclaiming and sharing its message, of praising God, and of instructing the faithful in the essentials of the faith.[7] "A confession is therefore faith moving into life and speech."[8] The Christian confession of faith in Christ "is oral, is public, and is heard"; it praises God publicly, and it is spoken to God in order to honor Him.[9]

Early in his career Martin Luther recognized the intimate connection between the confession of praise which Christians offer to describe God, the confession of sins which describes the repenting human creature who comes before Him, and the confession of faith, which describes both God and the sinner as it describes God's saving action in behalf of the sinner. All three acknowledge God as God, and all three are intended to bring benefit to the neighbor. " 'God is everything, the human creature nothing,' is the overarching expression for Luther's concept of confession, indeed, it is the basis for his whole piety. . . . Only out of this fundamental insight can the proper confession of sin arise for Luther. There is no more glorious confession of praise for God than the confession of our sin and weakness," according to Erich Vogelsang.[10] Believers proceed from the confession of sins to the confession of praise and the confession of faith.

The roots of Christian confession extend back to the praise of Yahweh in the Old Testament as well as to the New Testament testimony that Jesus of Nazareth was God in the flesh, crucified, and risen from the dead. Early Christian confessions responded first to the Jews' objections and then to the Gentiles' against the church's claim that Jesus was Lord, Yahweh in the flesh (John 20:28; 1 Cor. 12:3).[11]

Faith produces confession and must express itself, for trust in God always displays itself in word and deed (Acts 3:20; Rom. 10:9–15). Christian confession of faith is always dependent on, initiated by, and a response to the Word of God, arising out of God's pledge of Himself to those who are baptized. Confession is a response of thanks and praise to God's faithfulness.[12] Public voicing of the faith in confession produces and elicits faith, and it can also become the norm of faith, as it guides other believers in their own expression of their faith. Confession is literally "from faith and for faith" whenever the dynamic power of God's Good News is restated in human words (Rom. 1:16–17). Rationalistic philosophizing loses its absolute dominance when faith asserts itself in confession,[13] though reason can and will support faith if permitted its proper ministerial rather than a magisterial role. Since God the Holy Spirit elicits human confession of His Word, the process of expressing the faith in actual fact stands under His control, not under the control of the creature (1 Cor. 12:3).[14]

The purpose of confessing is always to bear testimony to God's message to humanity.[15] The purpose of this study is to understand the nature of confession in the 16th century, how it developed, and the reason for it.

God's message can be defined not only by positive assertions of what God has told His people but also by negative statements that demarcate God's truth from human perversion and error. Lutherans in the 16th century believed that both positive and negative statements were necessary. Later generations of Christians have sometimes questioned the method and the sometimes unnecessarily harsh tone of some confession. But the condemnation of false teaching has been a part of Christian confession from the time of the earliest church. Such condemnation is necessary for preserving truth and harmony within the church and for warning those who might be beguiled by error.[16] What Armin-Ernst Buchrucker says about the Formula of Concord is and has been true of all confessions: They divide as well as gather. They create not just harmony but a community in harmony, a people called to be one by the Word of God. Such a community is based on a common understanding of the truth of God's Word and a common understanding of how God's Word is to be applied in specific situations and on specific issues.[17] When such a common understanding breaks down, the harmony of God's church begins to collapse.

From the early confessions that Jesus is Lord and Christ (Acts 2:36), through the creeds of the patristic period and medieval conciliar decrees, the church always expressed its faith publicly, echoing the earlier confessions of faith and always anchoring its confession in Scripture. Not only was the content important but also the act of confessing—particularly the heroic confessions of martyrs (both ancient and modern).

From Augsburg to the Lutheran Church

The confession at Augsburg provided the confessors' churches and their heirs with a statement of how the faith was and would continue to be believed, taught, and confessed. By confessing the faith at the imperial diet, the princes and municipal representatives also placed their witness to the Gospel on the political/secular agenda of the Holy Roman Empire. Their confession became a tool for addressing the exigencies imposed on German political structures by religious division. But far more important, it returned to the original definition of the Christian church as a confessing body of believers who hear and repeat the Word of God (instead of church understood as an organic hierarchy). Augsburg gave new meaning to the word *confession*.

In the 19th century, the Brothers Grimm still defined the German noun *Bekenntnis* (confession) as an act or activity—confessing.[18] But long before the Grimms, *confession* had become synonymous with *document* (though it took some time before the "Augsburg Confession" was viewed primarily as a document). The Lutheran leaders at Augsburg performed their act of confession with a written document, presenting a handwritten copy to the emperor and then printing copies for distribution. Other Christians followed their example and composed formal confessional documents to express their faith publicly.

The written confession served not only as a symbol of the faith but also as a legal definition which regulated the church's life and its place in society, particularly in relation to the government. As

David Hollaz, a prominent dogmatician at the turn of the 18th century stated, the Lutheran confessions would (among other things) "furnish an account of the Christian religion, if it be demanded by the civil authorities."[19]

Thus, in Europe, the word *confession* soon came to denote roughly what North Americans call a denomination, a "church or body of Christians having a particular confession of faith." To be sure, other Christians have different views of their formal confessions of faith from those of Lutherans.[20] Yet the Roman Catholic scholar Walter Zeeden entitled his work on the development of the different churches (including his own) *The Origin of the Confessions.*[21] He comments that the creation of "confessional" groups arose "certainly without wishing for it, out of the Evangelical movement and the Catholic reform which it elicited." The process included the spiritual and administrative consolidation of these "confessional" movements into ecclesiastical institutions that were at least semi-stable in dogma and organization. This process arose in the first place from confessors and their confessions. First among these 16th-century confessors were the Lutherans who submitted their confession to the emperor at Augsburg in 1530.[22] Their confession created a new mode of designating distinct groups within Western Christendom. By the 17th century the Lutherans returned to the practice of the medieval church in its public and official proclamation of the Word by depending on the works of prominent theologians. They left the confessional writings of the 16th century to be *symbolic* in more than one sense.[23] This relative neglect of their confessions in the process of theological formulation does not alter the fact, however, that the Lutherans themselves, and other groups within western Christendom, came to think of their churches as *confessions.*

Recently, scholars have focused on the formation of these confessional groups as an important factor in the development of early modern Europe. This process of "confessionalization" was, according to Heinz Schilling, "a fundamental process in society, which ploughed up the public and private life of Europe in thoroughgoing fashion." Schilling does not ignore the theological aspects of this process of reorganizing Western European society in the late 16th and early 17th centuries. However, from his perspective, the similarities among the Lutherans, Roman Catholics, and

Calvinists of the period were greater than their differences—in theology and piety and also in the legal institutional forms of church life. Schilling focuses on the correlations and contradictions between ecclesiastical developments and the new forms of political and social life in the early modern period. Both on the local level and on the imperial level this process of "confessionalization" continued as governments tried to construct the absolutist state and as churches defended their own teachings and practices.[24]

Luther's followers at Augsburg were probably not unaware that their confession would be linked to larger societal forces. Primarily, however, they were simply responding to the emperor's request to define and defend their practice of Christianity. Hindsight views this confession of faith by Luther's followers as a natural means of defining themselves. In fact, such a self-definition did grow naturally out of the theological and historical development of the early years of the Wittenberg Reformation. But issuing a confession of faith was not the only possible course of action for Lutheran leaders at Augsburg, as noted above.

Confession Based on the Living Word

Martin Luther believed that God had selected certain specific elements of His created order, such as the human nature of Jesus of Nazareth, to convey His recreating power in human life and history. The divine Word of God was expressed in human language as well as in Jesus' flesh (John 1:14), and that Word was more than just a sign pointing to a heavenly reality. Human language, as the "living voice of the Gospel," in Luther's words, conveys the actual power of God into the human situation (Rom. 1:16). This word accomplishes God's will (Is. 55:10–11) as a living, active instrument, comparable to a sword (Heb. 4:12).[25] For Luther, the church and God's people live under the power of the Word. Georg Heckel has summarized Luther's view:

> The Gospel is the living Word of God to us, which God let take form (*persona*) among us in Jesus Christ. Through Him and the witnesses whom He has called, this Word, which is full of life and which creates life, is proclaimed. The church is founded on the Gospel, on the living voice of the Gospel, on the "oral shout" of Jesus Christ (WA 40,II,37; 411,1). Where this living Word of God

is on the move, there is life, salvation, and blessing. The Gospel is a living voice, the Word of God is a life-giving word."[26]

From Luther's perspective, the Gospel recounts *and* conveys God's action. Proclaiming, teaching, and confessing the Gospel is a human work, a good work commanded by God. Faith in Christ is God's gift. The confession of the faith is a fruit of faith and a result of the Holy Spirit sanctifying the believer's life.[27]

Luther believed that in giving life, salvation, and blessing to His people, this Word of God always calls God's people to express their God-given unity by drawing them into the body of Christ.[28] At the same time, confessing God's Word also must introduce "separation, judgment, and condemnation" into the church, for it serves as "a normative reference and critical instrument" for determining the church's life under the power of the Holy Spirit.[29] The Spirit continually calls the church back to the Word through the Word, since the Word is the normative reference and critical instrument to preserve God's message for His people.[30] Luther acknowledged that the expression of God's message develops—as it did, for instance, in the church's formulation of the dogma of the Trinity.[31] Formulations of the same essential content may change because of a different context. Asian and African cultures may greet the Gospel of Jesus Christ with age-old presuppositions that twist Western theological terminology, such as *justification*, as the term is adapted into a new cultural context. Even within Anglo-American culture the term *justification* in the popular mind has changed since the 16th century. Therefore, terminology may have to be changed in differing geographical, cultural, and historical situations. But the message itself remains the same. For the message is not merely a system of thought nor even a story told for its own sake. The message introduces a person, Jesus Christ, who is God in human flesh.

Confessing and Teaching the Word

Luther firmly believed that the Word of God always brings Christ into contact with human lives.[32] Faith in God's Word is inseparably connected with faith in Jesus Christ. Faith is the bridge between the truth of God as revealed in Christ and the believer who confesses. Therefore, truth and confession of the faith belong together. Luther assumed that the faith which is confessed is true.[33] He did not have a relative view of truth (a major presupposition of contemporary Western culture!). He was convinced that God has given His church "an objective, binding Christian truth, which is contained in the Holy Scripture *independent of the way in which it is understood at any given time* (emphasis added). It can be formulated into binding doctrine and differentiated from false doctrine. It may claim authority against arbitrary subjectivity." This authority of the truth has been passed down since the time of the apostles, although alloyed by deviations. This truth implies the unity of all Christians and rejects the possibility of pluralism of confessional *content* (a point on which Christians today are sometimes confused).[34]

This truth presents the person of Christ. It is found only in Holy Scripture. "In a qualified sense one can speak of a Real Presence of Christ in the Word of the Scripture in Luther's thought ... just because the Word of Scripture is no empty word, nor just a word which offers a promise." Instead, it is a "word which delivers what it talks about."[35] For Luther, this Scripture is the only source, rule, and norm of faith, for faith is faith in Christ. What God has said in Christ is all He has to say. The Scriptures tell His people all they need to know of Christ. They are forever sufficient in what they have revealed about God.[36]

Luther repeatedly made clear his reliance on the authority and power of Scripture. Citing Bernard, Augustine, and Jerome, he wrote in *On the Councils and the Church* that, in Augustine's words, Scripture alone cannot err. Luther concluded, "If it had not been for Holy Scripture, the church, had it depended on the councils and fathers, would not have lasted long."[37] Luther believed in the clarity of Scripture as one facet of its authority. He also believed in the corruptibility of every human authority that attempts to interpret it. Therefore, Luther believed that the entire life of those who proclaim the Word of God must be one of repentance.

Despite the shortcomings and sins of those who interpret Scripture, Luther insisted that the Bible's message must be proclaimed to all the saints. For the power of the Word to condemn and to restore—to kill our sinful nature and to make us new people alive in Christ—is conveyed only when the Word is proclaimed. This means that God's people must continuously confess and teach the faith. For confessing the faith means interpreting and applying the

Scriptures to contemporary life.[38] In this sense, confessing the faith is almost synonymous with teaching the faith.

The concept of teaching, or doctrine, became vital for the Wittenberg reformers. Melanchthon taught the faith by organizing doctrine into topics (in Latin, *loci*). Organizing into topics led to a certain quantification of the Biblical message. Luther did not oppose Melanchthon's method. Some scholars believe that this approach diluted the power of the Word of God in later Lutheran theology.[39] However, it was inevitable that the church would divide the teaching of the Bible into topics as it sought to answer various questions and study specific subjects in the Bible. The power of God's Word remained the vital center of Luther's understanding of it. He never tired of proclaiming the Word because he believed that through preaching, teaching, and confessing it God's power is set loose in the world.

The reformers at Wittenberg focused on both the content of the confession and the activity of conveying the content. Peter Fraenkel has used the term *verbal noun* to explain Philip Melanchthon's use of *doctrina, traditio,* and *ministerium* (doctrine, tradition, and ministry). Verbal nouns are nouns that designate an "activity, function, or process."[40] Thus, for example, Melanchthon (and Luther too) understood *teaching* to be both the content and the activity of teaching that content. The Wittenberg reformers viewed confessing the faith in the same way, as both what is confessed and the act of confessing, as we shall see in Chapter Two. They would have agreed that

> form and content ... cannot be separated. One cannot divorce faith as an act of believing from the faith that is believed. A confession is, in fact, that which is being confessed here and now. An act of confessing, can, of course, become a past completed event and therefore a confession. But in so far as a past confession remains, or becomes again, a living, present event, it is the content of an act of confession today.[41]

Hermann Sasse called attention to the implications of this understanding of confession for the Lutheran church when he was pressured by the Third Reich not to make a clear confession:

> The Evangelical Lutheran Church is not an idea. It is a reality. It is not dumb, but speaks. For it would not be a church if it had

23

not borne witness, if it did not continue to bear witness, to what
it is—what it is particularly as a *Lutheran* church.[42]

Confession and the Creeds

Luther acknowledged the importance of confessional documents
throughout his ministry. In 1538 he published a brief treatment of
"the three symbols or confessions of the Christian faith," the Apostles
Creed, the Athanasian Creed, and the Te Deum Laudamus. At the
end of his treatise he added the Nicene Creed, which he usually
regarded as chief among the standards for teaching and confession.
These creeds or confessions summarized the faith in a manner that
could be taught to children and uneducated people. The creeds
served as "protectors" of the faith, for "in all histories of Christendom ... all those who have correctly had and kept the chief article
of Jesus Christ have remained safe and secure in the right Christian
faith." Luther viewed these ancient confessions as "secondary authorities"—what later Lutheran dogmaticians called a *norma normata,* or a norm which stands under a primary norm. He could do
so because he believed that these confessions were derived from
the Scriptures, rested firmly on Biblical revelation, and conveyed
the Word of God from the Scriptures to the people of his day.[43]

Explanations of the Nicene Creed were also published by those
in Melanchthon's inner circle to help the church use it as a secondary
authority. Caspar Cruciger, a student and colleague of both Luther
and Melanchthon, wrote that such symbols were established within
the church so that both the unlearned and the learned might have
a source of reliable teaching readily available to them and so they
might be instructed in this confession of the faith.[44]

For Luther and his followers, to be confessional meant not only
to accept the content of documents which properly present the
Biblical truth, but also to confess, to set that truth winsomely before
the people who frequent the marketplace and who engage in the
political discussion and decision-making of society. It was also natural for Luther to confess the faith publicly because of his understanding of the way in which the confessed Word creates faith in
its hearers. Furthermore, it was natural for him to confess the faith
by condemning false doctrine. He believed that sin and evil spring

24

ultimately from doubting God's Word. The doubt and deception in false teaching must be labeled and countered. Therefore, Luther's followers did what came naturally to them when they were invited to confess the Word of the Lord at Augsburg.

Lutherans Learn to Confess

If the Lutheran church was born confessing at Augsburg, it was conceived at Wittenberg in the matrix of the venerable genre of the scholastic disputation. Luther's scholastic education had trained him to assert ideas publicly and to contrast them with the ideas of others. Such academic contests quickly turned from sport to war. Luther challenged the indulgence system in 1517, and thereafter he was quickly cast into the role of a confessor. Before the papal representative Cardinal Cajetan at the Diet of Augsburg in 1518 and Emperor Charles V at the Diet of Worms in 1521, he faced the same question that the Roman officials had posed for the ancient martyrs—and the same question we often face today as people and causes vie for our attention and allegiance: Who, ultimately, is our Lord? Emperor Charles V claimed lordship—albeit a qualified lordship—over Western Christian society, even lordship over its faith. Luther just said no, however, and confessed Jesus Christ alone as Lord.

Luther against Erasmus: The Assertion of the Faith

Nowhere is Luther's zeal for public confession clearer than in his debate with Erasmus. Some have suggested that their definitions of the nature of the theological task were as much an issue in their debate as the freedom or bondage of the human will (the topic of Erasmus' 1524 attack on Luther in his *Freedom of the Will*).

Erasmus believed that great truths are more or less accessible to all; Luther believed that only the Word of God can reveal the truth of God to people because we are all shrouded in sin. Erasmus believed that the presence of Christ and the Holy Spirit preserve the church from grievous error; Luther believed that Satan is always at work causing believers to err and that error must always be confronted with bold confession. Luther's position was clear:

25

> It is not the mark of a Christian mind to take no delight in asser-
> tions; on the contrary, a man must delight in assertions or he will
> be no Christian. And by assertion—in order that we may not be
> misled by words—I mean a constant adhering, affirming, con-
> fessing, maintaining, and an invincible persevering. . . . Nothing is
> better known or more common among Christians than assertion.
> Take away assertions and you take away Christianity.[45]

Gottfried Krodel has observed that for Luther theology was *affirmation,* i.e., *assertio,* and that the practice of theology was a con-
fesssional task. Krodel suggests that upholding the confessional
nature of theology and doing theology distinguishes Luther from
Erasmus, and the controversy about the freedom of the will was
only a manifestation of this fundamental difference in their views.
Erasmus saw theology as a descriptive task, establishing the norm
of Christian existence; but for Luther, theology was a confessional
activity "by which the [very] existence of man was shaped."[46] The
significance of this dispute is noted by Ulrich Asendorf:

> *Assertio* and justifying faith on the one side and on the other
> skepticism, which relies on reason and the power of the free will,
> stand alongside each other as mutually exclusive antitheses. This
> highlights the tension between the two poles of modern thought.
> Enlightened reason continually refines and cultivates skepticism.
> It has become a leitmotiv of modern scholarship—indeed, quite
> plainly, its fundamental criterion for thought—as it finds its classic
> expression in Kant's "Critiques." The theology of successive gen-
> erations—right up to the present—has been torn back and forth
> between *assertio* and skepticism, not the least for this reason:
> because the scholarly nature of its methods stands and falls with
> its commitment to skepticism. Luther, by contrast, takes the po-
> sition that *assertio* is the only appropriate form for theological
> existence.[47]

Erasmus anticipated the descriptive approach to theology, which
attempts to maintain control over its subject rather than react in
faith to it. In contrast to Erasmus' descriptive method, Luther's approach remained outside that which is academically domesticable.
It fits the dynamics of the pulpit, but it fits less well into the rational
confines of the podium. It was as if the Greek philosophers and the
Hebrew prophets were at war. Luther did not believe that the Word
of God could be analyzed and dissected in the same way that reason

could analyze the subject of creation. He believed that God's Word ought simply be proclaimed. The response of faith is different from that of reason. Faith believes and cannot help but teach and confess.

Luther responded with the assertion of his confession of faith when challenged by Zwingli, Carlstadt, and others on the issue of the real presence of Christ's body and blood in the Lord's Supper. Luther entitled his most important treatise on this issue *Confession Concerning Christ's Supper* and concluded it with a doctrinal last will and testament. In it he expressed "my faith" on a wide range of teaching that had been disputed for a decade. He did not view this confession as merely the statement of one Christian. He was conscious of his role as a doctor of the church, and he intended his confession to be a formal exercise of that office to which God had called him and to which he was bound: to teach and to confess. Luther confessed from the same eschatological perspective which he considered inherent in all Christian confession:

> I desire with this treatise to confess my faith before God and all the world, point by point. I am determined to abide by it until my death and (so help me God!) in this faith to depart from this world and to appear before the judgment seat of our Lord Jesus Christ.[48]

This conclusion to his *Confession* was a prime source for the writing of the Augsburg Confession.

Four Concrete Needs for Public Confession

Luther's personal confessional stance during the first decade of the Reformation found parallels in the larger events surrounding his movement. Gottfried Seebass has identified four reasons why Luther and his followers felt it necessary to formulate a public confession of what they believed.

First, Luther and others felt compelled to translate Luther's ideas, composed in an academic setting, into forms that could be used for the teaching and preaching of his message. Melanchthon, for instance, published his *Loci communes* (or "topics of Christian teaching") not so much for confession as for instruction, but nonetheless as a public presentation of his ideas. Seebass includes documents

27

like the Saxon Visitation Articles of 1528 and Luther's catechisms in this category of quasi-confessional writings.

Second, the Reformation movement that was spreading rapidly in early 16th century Germany demanded some explanation or defense before the political authorities. In various lands and cities, Evangelical preachers stepped before their magistrates to offer an *apologia* for their faith. The *Protestatio* of the Evangelical princes at the imperial diet in Speyer in 1529, from which the title *Protestant* arose, was this same kind of defense. (*Protestatio* meant *testimony,* not *protest,* in the Latin of that day.)

Third, Luther and his followers had to confess their faith when confronted by those with alternate proposals for reform in the church. Many of their opponents followed the model set forth by the biblicistic, moralistic, anti-clerical, anti-sacramental and often millennialistic sects of the Middle Ages, and they disagreed sharply on at least some points with the Lutherans' teaching.

Fourth, some princes committed themselves to the Lutheran movement and therefore placed themselves under the threat of the emperor's edict against the Lutherans at Worms. These princes needed to define the basis on which they might ally with one another for the defense of their common faith.[49] The Schwabach Articles, which Melanchthon used in composing the first 21 articles of the Augsburg Confession, is an example of such a doctrinal basis for an alliance of Lutheran political leaders.

The details of the development of the text of the Augsburg Confession after the followers of Luther arrived in Augsburg has been described at length elsewhere and need not be detailed here.[50] Significantly, Melanchthon originally regarded the document he was shaping as an *apology,* a defense of Evangelical practices for the emperor who had demanded to know why the Evangelical princes were disobeying the Edict of Worms. However, the attacks of Roman Catholic theologians on the fundamental teaching of the Wittenbergers led Melanchthon to reshape his document into a public confession of the catholic faith. He believed the Wittenberg movement was faithfully teaching the doctrinal content of Scripture.[51] It is noteworthy that the attacks on the Lutherans did not cause them to be more defensive, but instead caused them to go on the offensive with a public confession of their faith. Melanchthon and his colleagues made this public confession with trepidation but also with a joyful confidence in the power of the Word of God.

The Augsburg Confession was intended as a call to the whole church for repentance and unity in the Gospel. However, it immediately became the charter and birth certificate of the Lutheran Reformation and the churches to which it gave birth throughout Europe. As such a charter, it expresses what the founders of this Reformation thought the church is and what the church should be.

The Augsburg Confessors

The particular people who confessed at Augsburg reveal much about the Lutherans' understanding of the church. The Confession read at Augsburg on June 25, 1530, came from the pen of a theologian, Philip Melanchthon. Though never ordained into the clergy, he was a learned scholar of Scripture and a Biblical humanist who prized good rhetoric. A correct understanding of the Biblical message and effective communication of that message were of ultimate importance in Melanchthon's eyes. He composed the Confession with considerable aid from pastors and professors, including Luther. Though Luther was safely ensconced beyond the reach of the emperor's police at the Coburg, he still exercised influence on his colleagues at Augsburg.[52] Melanchthon was also advised by lay people as he polished the text of the Confession. It was presented as the confession of lay people, specifically, of the princes of the empire who had been summoned by Charles V to give an account of their faith. They did just that; and in doing so, they invited Charles to join them in this confession.

Confessors, Lay and Ordained

Traditionally, the clergy had spoken in public for the church; and since 1530, clergy have generally been the ones to voice the church's message to the world. The Council of Nicea (A.D. 325) may have been Emperor Constantine's show, but its decrees and its creed also came from the theologians. But, very significantly, at this key point in the Lutheran Reformation, lay people—whom Luther called *priests*—told the emperor and his people, "This is the Word of the Lord; listen to it." They did so in part because they believed that all baptized Christians are priests of God who have free access to God

29

and have the privilege of proclaiming God's Word to others. Luther, in his 1520 *Open Letter to the Christian Nobility,* had argued in behalf of their *right* to proclaim.[53] But more than that, the laymen saw that, in their situation, confession was necessary because the legitimacy of their ecclesiastical reforms was being challenged on the basis of the law of the land, by the Theodosian Code which stated that "the doctrine of the Gospel" must be taught by those who wished to remain within the Roman law.[54] Hence the confession of their faith had political as well as religious ramifications.

The confessing princes of 1530 also stood before the emperor and the empire because they believed that God had called them to serve the spiritual needs of their people. Luther had taught that all activities in the secular and temporal realms were God-pleasing when done out of true faith. The princes who published *The Book of Concord* in their own names a half-century later reflected the same sense of responsibility the confessors at Augsburg had felt when they stated the following:

> We are mindful of the responsibility that we have by divine pre-
> cept, on account of the office we hold, over against the temporal
> and eternal welfare of our own selves and of the subjects who
> belong to us, to do and to continue to do everything that is useful
> and profitable to the increase and expansion of God's praise and
> glory, to the propagation of that Word of His which alone brings
> salvation, to the tranquillity and peace of Christian schools and
> churches, and to the needed consolation and instruction of poor,
> misguided consciences.[55]

Lutherans in other places and times may understand the responsibility of governing officials differently, in accordance with Luther's distinction of the two realms, the earthly and the heavenly. Yet the principle that God has commissioned all *believers* as confessors and caretakers of fellow-believers stands as an integral part of the theology which Luther bequeathed his heirs.

The Agenda at Augsburg

The confessors at Augsburg, lay people and theologians alike, came there for a discussion of the reform of the church. They found themselves in a situation in which they felt compelled to confess their faith. The content of their confession was of utmost importance to them, for they believed it was both the truth and the power of God. Even though Melanchthon originally intended to defend only the practice of the reforming principalities—as he and his Wittenberg colleagues had planned when they drafted the Torgau Articles the previous March—the Lutherans also came to Augsburg ready to explain their doctrinal positions and to confess the teaching which they held to be faithful to the Scriptures.[56] Emperor Charles V had demanded that the Lutheran princes justify their rejection of papal supremacy in the church. The confessors explained their refusal to submit to the church of Rome by

> offering and presenting a confession of our pastors' and preachers' teaching and of our own faith, setting forth how and in what manner, on the basis of the Holy Scriptures, these things are preached, taught, communicated, and embraced in our lands.[57]

This confession made no claim to authority apart from the authority of Scripture.[58] All it claimed to do was to announce and apply the Biblical message to the specific questions of its day.

Melanchthon and his fellow confessors were anxious to demonstrate that they were in the catholic tradition of confessing the faith that extended back to the ancient church. They were not running from the marketplace but were claiming their rightful place within the Christian culture of Europe. They insisted on the right to be included in the unity of the faith as defined by the Theodosian Code. Hence the Confession anchors its first article in the faith of Nicea, and it frequently appeals to condemnations voiced by the ancient fathers and occasionally to Augustine as well. Article 7 in particular affirmed that the Lutherans were not sectarian heretics but had every right to be identified as full members of Christ's church.[59] The confessors were certain that their "teaching is grounded clearly on Holy Scripture and is not contrary or opposed to that of the univeral Christian church or even to that of the Roman church (in so far as its teaching is reflected in the writings of the [ancient] fathers)."[60]

Confessing the Faith of the Church

The confessors did not confess just for the sake of confessing or as an exercise of personal whim. Instead, they sought to be instruments of God as He recreated His people. God recreates through His Word, the same Word which brought the universe into existence. This Word was not a word of magic but of meaning. The Word is true, and all that opposes it is false. The confessors sought unity on the basis of the "one single Christian truth."[61] The "one true religion" unites Christ's people "under one Christ" and leads them to "confess and contend for Christ."[62]

The faith of Luther and the confessors at Augsburg was Christocentric without being Christomonistic. The fourth and fundamental Lutheran *sola*, the *solus Christus,* does not reduce the Biblical message to simple pieties regarding Jesus. According to the Augsburg Confession, "Christ alone" does not complete but rather permeates the teaching of the church, as the church has always confessed.[63]

Werner Elert has observed a parallel between the structure of the Smalcald Articles and the Augsburg Confession in the presentation of the faith. The Smalcald Articles began with "the sublime articles of the divine majesty" which were not matters of dispute or contention since both parties confessed them. Part I of the Smalcald Articles parallels the first article of the Augsburg Confession, in which Melanchthon established the catholicity of the Lutherans by confessing the doctrine of the Trinity. Part II of the Smalcald Articles "treats the articles which pertain to the office and work of Jesus Christ, or to our redemption," the subject of Augsburg Confession articles 3 and 4 (article 2 treats the need for Christ's saving work in its discussion of original sin). Luther's focus in the second part of the Smalcald Articles is different from Melanchthon's in the Augsburg Confession, but the underlying teaching and concerns are the same. The Smalcald Articles then continue with Part III, dealing with issues on which there may be discussion (though not compromise) "with learned and sensible men." Part III touches on some of the topics which the remainder of the Augsburg Confession deals with, and so the two are parallel in this respect.[64]

The Roman Confutation accepted Article 3 of the Augsburg Confession, which deals with the person and work of Christ and the Holy Spirit's work in bringing Christ's benefits to the church. However, the Roman Confutation's critique of Article 4 on justification provoked a massive response from Melanchthon. Readers of the Augsburg Confession often overlook the critical role of Article 3 because of its acceptance by the Roman Confutation. These two articles set the groundwork for the rest of the confession. The article on justification simply defines more sharply the article on the work of Christ and the Holy Spirit. The confession of the Triune God (Article 1) and the acknowledgment of human sinfulness (Article 2) proclaim God's saving work in the incarnation and in the gift of faith in Christ which the Holy Spirit brings to believers (Article 3). As Nicea had protested the domestication of the Biblical scandal of the cross regarding the person of Jesus Christ, so Augsburg was a formal protest against those who subtly and not so subtly misrepresented the work of Christ.

Article 5 says that to obtain such faith, God instituted the ministry of the means of grace. Article 6 says that out of such faith come good works. The means of grace constitute the church, the assembly of all believers (Articles 7 and 8), and those means of grace and their use are discussed in Articles 9-14. The church lives out its life in the means of grace with the aid of human customs, the subject of Article 15, and its people live in human society, the subject of Article 16. The Confession concludes with a brief treatment of several other topics important to the Evangelicals in 1530, including elements of church life crying out for reform.

Confessing the Faith in Context

The confession of the "one single Christian truth" did not attempt to describe the whole Christian truth in every detail. It confessed the Biblical message in reaction to the challenges of its age. The church must always confess its faith in the Triune God, the work of Christ, and the activity of the Holy Spirit. Yet the church's confession always must answer the concerns raised by the contemporary world. The articles of faith which the confessors at Augsburg set forth were not selected because they were Melanchthon's 21 favorite doctrines. He chose his topics in response to the issues raised by the Lutherans' opponents.

The absence of a description of theological presuppositions perhaps weakens the Confession in one sense, for without a good grasp of its authors' conceptual framework it could be misunderstood. The reader of the Confession needs to be familiar with Luther's understanding of God as Creator, the goodness of creation, God's use of creation in saving His people, the distinction between the two kinds of human righteousness (that which the human creature performs and that which God gives for Christ's sake through faith)— and the corollary of this distinction, the proper distinction of Law and Gospel, and the theology of the cross. The reader of the Confession must have some acquaintance with these doctrines because the words of the Confession can be forced to fit other false conceptual frameworks that twist the beliefs affirmed in the Confession. The confessors assumed that their audience would understand their theological presuppositions, but one cannot assume that people today either recognize or share those presuppositions.

The presentation of the Augsburg Confession had a twofold goal: Christian instruction, and the consolation of troubled consciences. Melanchthon was always concerned with the troubled or tender conscience. For example, in Article 11 of the Apology, while discussing confession and absolution, Melanchthon rejoiced that "we have so explained and extolled the blessing of absolution and the power of the keys that many troubled consciences have received consolation from our teaching." Melanchthon criticized fasting regulations because "such traditions have turned out to be a grievous burden to consciences" (AC 26, 12). The confessors believed that it was necessary to pursue the two goals of education and consolation so that they would not put their souls "in grave peril before God by misusing His name or Word, nor should we wish to bequeath to our children and posterity any other teaching than that which agrees with the pure Word of God and Christian truth." Their teaching, they believed, "is grounded clearly on the Holy Scriptures and is not contrary or opposed to that of the universal Christian church, or even of the Roman church."[65] Unfortunately, the Roman church disagreed. But this confession of the truth delivered God's Word to sinners so that they might live in the consolation of the Gospel of Jesus Christ. This is why the Lutherans confessed with joy and confidence.

The Purpose of the Augsburg Confession

Hermann Sasse has noted that God's revelation of Himself first prompted the church to confess its faith. Confession is faith's answer to the received Word of God. Second, it is the response of the church, the believers collectively, not only of the individual believer. Third, it is a part of the liturgy, "in the divine service, in which the church appears as the hearing, praying, and confessing congregation."[66]

Georg Heckel distinguishes two kinds of public confession of faith in the ancient church: the "dogmatic-limiting confession," and the "liturgical-catechetical confession." The Augsburg Confession originally was presented to the emperor as an expression of the teaching and practice of the churches. Subsequently, it was also used as a dogmatic and limiting confession. Although the Augsburg Confession was never a liturgical-catechetical confession in the same sense as the ancient creeds, it did grow out of the worship and catechetical instruction of the churches. "Not only the teaching but also the life and action of the church in its practical exercise was made visible to the estates of the empire through the formulation of the Augsburg Confession."[67] The confessors could not help but reveal the liturgical and catechetical life of their churches as they set forth their faith.

This Biblical, catholic faith which the confessors presented in their Confession could be expressed differently when addressing different issues. Melanchthon and his colleagues chose to express their faith in parallel confessions in German and Latin, neither of which was simply a translation of the other. Because the Latin-speaking audience had some concerns different from the German-speaking audience, they used different wording, appropriate for each audience.

Though the differences in the two versions of the Confession may be minimal, they do indicate that, for the Lutherans, the *meaning* of the Biblical message was what was important. The specific wording could differ according to the audience and situation.[68] In no way does this suggest that "many are the ways to one God" or that there can be contradictory expressions of the one Biblical truth. It only affirms that the message of Scripture must be communicated in understandable and relevant forms. The Lutheran Confessions are not exhaustive expositions of the Biblical message, but they are clear expressions of the Biblical teachings that applied to the questions being debated at the time they were written.

The concerns addressed in the Augsburg Confession were concerns of all German society. The Augsburg Confession is basic if one is to appreciate what Luther and his followers believed the nature of confession to be. They believed that the message of Jesus Christ must be voiced in the marketplace and in the public forum. So the confessors proclaimed Jesus Christ and His justifying love in the economic center of the empire, in the midst of the imperial estates. It was appropriate for them to do so, for it was a place in which their confession would be heard.

Stepping Softly for the Sake of Unity

The confessors were determined to confess persuasively. They did not simply throw their statements at the emperor and the estates of the empire, but they chose their words carefully so that even their enemies might listen. The primary function of the condemnations contained in the Augsburg Confession was to clarify the confessors' message, but they also had the secondary function of establishing common ground with those who condemned the same opponents.[69] One of Luther's famous remarks regarding Melanchthon's "soft-stepping" (Leisetreterei) actually expresses their common concern that the Confession be persuasive. Luther occasionally disapproved of Melanchthon's approach. But this phrase, often quoted to demonstrate Luther's disapproval, appears quite different in context: "I have read Master Philip's Apologia [the Augsburg Confession], and it pleases me very much. I know of nothing to improve or change in it, and that would not be appropriate anyway, for I cannot tread so softly and gently as he."[70] Even when there was little chance that they would win over their opponents, Luther and Melanchthon both wanted their message to be as persuasive as possible.

The confessors at Augsburg confessed their faith because the emperor had commanded them to explain why they had defied his edict against the Lutheran reform movement. Their confession created a new legal precedent for the Holy Roman Empire. The concept of a religious confession became an integral part of German life.[71] At another diet in Augsburg, 25 years later, the Religious Peace was established on the basis of the Augsburg Confession.

The confessors also issued their confession because of a sense of eschatological urgency. Luther firmly believed that Christ would return to judge the world and bring this age to a close at any time.

He was convinced that the hours available to bring God's message of forgiveness of sins to people were few and limited. This conviction impelled him to bold confession. Although Melanchthon tended to moderate Luther's stress on the nearness of the end of all things, the Augsburg Confession treated "the return of Christ to judgment" in Article 17 and treated the Holy Spirit's bestowal of new life through faith in Article 3 from the perspective of the approaching end of all things.[72]

The confessors came to Augsburg with a strong concern for Christian unity, and the Augsburg Confession urged all Christians to pursue unity in the faith. The confessors came prepared to discuss practical ways to restore the unity of the church, hoping that their discussions might reconcile the differences and unite all in one true religion, "even as we are all under one Christ and should confess and contend for Christ." They believed that the unity of the church depends on "agreement on one Christian truth, [putting] aside whatever may not have been rightly interpreted or treated *by either side* [emphasis added], to have all of us embrace and adhere to a single, true religion and live together in unity and in one fellowship and church, even as we are all enlisted under one Christ."[73] To this end, the confessors at Augsburg issued their invitation to the church throughout the world to join them in confessing the Biblical faith. The next year, in 1531, the official version of the Confession appeared in print, though pirated editions had been produced by enterprising printers already in 1530.[74]

The Lutherans felt that the world had to know what to believe and also what to avoid believing. Therefore, in addition to teaching what is true, they followed the ancient practice of condemning false teaching. These condemnations were intended to aid the proclamation of the Gospel. In the Wittenberg Concord of 1536 Luther and his colleagues also condemned false teaching when they came to a common confession with Martin Bucer and the representatives of the south German and Swiss reformers.

The Lutherans did not condemn other Christians aimlessly. Even later, when the hostilities between the confessional groups in early modern Europe intensified, the successors of those at Augsburg issued condemnations in order to call to repentance those who disagreed. Still later, in the 17th century, Lutherans were often willing to invest a great deal of energy in colloquies with other confessional groups.[75] The spirit of Augsburg does not seek division or separation; its goal is rather to bring all Christians together under one confession of faith.

The Use of the Augsburg Confession

The heirs of the Augsburg confessors continued to be concerned primarily with identifying the truth of Scripture and confessing it. Yet the Augsburg Confession became more than an instrument for the proclamation of the Gospel. Ernst Koch has identified three major areas in which it served the church and European society: the secular, political realm; the realm of ecclesiastical discipline and order; and the realm of doctrinal authority within the church.[76]

A Defining Symbol

The Augsburg Confession acquired legal status as a definition of legitimate religion in the Holy Roman Empire after 1555. It also legitimized the Lutheran princes' political alliances after the Confession itself was legally sanctioned.[77]

The importance of the Confession as a *symbol*, in the sense of contributing a "brand name" for the Protestant estates of the German Empire, can be seen in the German Lutheran celebrations on the anniversaries of its presentation in Augsburg. These celebrations reflected their times as well as the varying status of the Confession. The first centennial fell during the dark days of the Thirty Years' War. On that occasion, the Lutheran estates asserted their determination to continue confessing the faith set forth at Augsburg.[78]

The Roman Catholic opponents of the Lutheran church were aware of the importance of the Augsburg Confession as a symbol of the movement. From the beginning, they recognized both its political and its ecclesiastical significance. The Confession served as a kind of lightning rod throughout the continuing battle for Lutheran political and ecclesiastical identity even beyond the 16th century.[79]

The Augsburg Confession professed to reflect "the teaching which is preached and taught in our churches for proper Christian instruction, the consolation of consciences, and the amendment of believers." It described the correction of abuses in the church by the Lutherans so that Charles V "may perceive that we have not acted in an unchristian and frivolous manner but have been compelled by God's command." The confessors were certain that Charles would "undoubtedly discover that the forms of teaching and of ceremonies observed among us are not so intolerable as those ungodly and malicious men represent."[80]

A Regulating Symbol

After 1530, the Augsburg Confession not only reflected but also regulated what was taught and practiced in the congregations of Lutheran churches. In some areas, it became a means of introducing the Reformation. As early as the 1530s, it was used to define what church life should be like at the parish level, for example, in the constitution of the Hessian church composed at Homburg. Through its use as a basis for examining pastors and candidates for the pastoral ministry and its use in Lutheran ordination vows, it continued to shape the life of the church at local and higher levels.[81]

A Normative Symbol

The Augsburg Confession began to play a third role as well: It became an authority within the church, an authority with no peer among human confessions but one which was totally subject to Scripture.

> The Gospel is the *norma normans* [the standard establishing the norm of what is to be believed]; and the confession of the church is the *norma normata* [the standard governed by the norma normans]. The identity of the Word of God and the confession of the church exists because (*quia*) both testify to the center of the faith: the salvation which God gives the human creature in Jesus Christ (CA 1–6).[82]

Lutherans gave their confessions the status of secondary authority (norma normata) in the church because they believed that these confessional documents faithfully reflect Scripture and are always to be tested by Scripture. Almost immediately Lutherans began using the Augsburg Confession to define the proper proclamation of God's Word.[83]

All Christian groups must have some authority for mediating

disputes and answering questions about the meaning of Scripture. The medieval church turned to councils and bishops, and especially to the pope, to answer questions and mediate disputes. After Scripture, the secondary authority to determine teaching lay with the councils and the pope.[84] Informal authority also rested in the writings of learned theologians, from Peter Lombard's time on particularly in their increasingly sophisticated dogmatic textbooks.

The Lutherans continued to use such informal authorities, but they replaced the medieval theologians with their own, including Luther, Martin Chemnitz, and the great dogmaticians of the 17th century. Initially, Luther himself served as a secondary authority, replacing the popes and councils. His followers could write to him or come to Wittenberg for an authoritative opinion from him or his colleagues. After Luther's death, many of his followers treated his writings as a standard for determining the proper interpretation of Scripture.[85]

By the end of the 16th century formal authority for interpretation of Scripture came to rest, for the Lutherans, in *The Book of Concord.* The Augsburg Confession remained the primary document within this collection of confessional documents. The disadvantage of using such documents as an authority is that the documents did not and could not address every question which might arise in the later life of the church. The advantage of such an organ for the exercise of secondary authority in the church is that the Book of Concord provides a model and an orientation for the teaching of the churches which accept it as a norma normata (*normed norm,* in the language of the 17th-century Lutheran teachers). The Book of Concord draws all its adherents into the active public confession of their faith in Jesus Christ. It orients their confession and teaching around Jesus Christ and the message of forgiveness and life which He is and brings.

Luther believed that the Word of God takes on living form as the words of the Gospel message spoken by Christ's disciples. Luther's understanding of God's Word enabled his followers to believe that a document such as a confession could be a secondary authority. As long as it was based on Scripture, a contemporary confession of faith in Jesus Christ could convey the power of God as it transmitted the Biblical message.

Philip Melanchthon's humanistic sensitivities supported the idea that authority could rest in a document. The Lutherans had a variety of other documents which could have served as authorities, such as teaching tools or dogmatic texts. But when Luther's catechisms came to be defined as formal authorities, they were grouped with documents labeled *confessions* and were themselves *called* confessions. After 1560, when individuals or churches endeavored to establish a larger group of authoritative documents, the entire collection was labeled a "body of teaching" (*corpus doctrinae*). Such a body of teaching consisted largely of documents that had come to be considered confessions.[86] The confessors at Augsburg had, however unconsciously, created a new form of secondary authority for the church in their confessional document.

Luther himself believed that the Augsburg Confession was sufficient to function as a norm. To be sure, Luther criticized Melanchthon's text because it conceded too much,[87] and because it did not discuss certain key issues such as purgatory and the pope.[88] But confessing the faith was Luther's style—and foremost interest.[89] He enthusiastically endorsed the Augsburg Confession as a "thoroughly magnificent confession," and he rejoiced to have "experienced the hour in which Christ was proclaimed with such a bold confession, publicly, before such an eminent assembly. This fulfilled the word, 'I will speak of your testimonies before kings' and will continue to fulfill what comes after that: 'And I was not put to shame' " (Ps. 119:48).[90]

Testifying before Kings

Luther was correct. His students continued to fulfill both parts of the psalm verse. His heirs came to appreciate confessing the faith as an integral and essential part of what it meant to be a believing Christian. Some of them, such as Hermann Sasse and Dietrich Bonhoeffer, would do so in the face of the demonic powers of the Third Reich. Others, such as the Salzburgers of the early 18th century or Paul Gerhardt in the late 17th, would do so in the face of persecution from other "confessions" of the Christian church. Still others, in the generation succeeding Luther's, would do so as they continued the process of establishing the Lutheran church as a confessing church, both in the face of Charles V's determination to enforce the Edict of Worms and in the face of temptations to apostasy arising in the wake of this imperial policy.

This study traces the development of the Lutherans' understanding of confessing the faith, as Luther's and Melanchthon's students saw it being modeled at Augsburg, as they worked to preserve their own confession in the wake of the emperor's efforts to suppress it in the years following the Smalcald War of 1546–47, and as they fashioned new confessions for new confessional situations.

The Model Confession: Augsburg 1530

It all went back to Augsburg. Throughout the 16th century, Luther's students and heirs looked back to Augsburg as the key to their confession of faith. They echoed Luther's appraisal of what happened there in 1530, as recorded by his faithful amanuensis, Georg Rörer. Luther must have shared this appraisal often during the last 15 years of his life, since his students frequently repeated slightly varying versions of it:

> The efficacy and power of God's Word is such that, the more it is persecuted, the more it flourishes and grows. Consider the diet at Augsburg, which was truly the final trumpet before the last day since the whole world was raging against God's Word. Oh, we had to pray that Christ himself would remain safe in heaven from the papists. At last, our teaching and faith came forth into the light through our confession, so that in a very brief time, by order of the emperor, it was sent to every king and prince. There were many bold men at the [imperial] court, whose enthusiasm for that teaching caught ablaze like tinder. Thus, our confession and defense were set forth with greatest glory. And their confutation groveled in the shadows [a reference to the Roman Catholic party's refusal to publish a copy of their Confutation of the Augsburg Confession or to permit Melanchthon and the other Evangelicals to see a copy of it]. Oh, how I wish that their confession had been produced in the light; how we would have liked to take that old tattered fur cloak and shake it so that the patches might have flown in every direction. But they hated the light. They did not want it out. We offered them peace and unity enough, but they very proudly refused to agree. Indeed, it was necessary for them to perish without mercy. Thus we read in [the book of] Joshua that Joshua offered peace to all the cities and none except Gibeon accepted; all the rest he struck down, and they perished without

mercy. For these reasons that diet of ours was worthy of praise. No one should regret what happened there. For the Word of God was entered as evidence against the opinion of emperor, pope, and the Epicureans. They wanted to smother it, but it arose and sallied forth.[1]

Naive as it may have been in some respects, Luther's understanding of the confession at Augsburg was shared by his Lutheran contemporaries. This common view developed as the Lutherans were preparing their presentation at the diet, and it influenced Luther's students throughout the following half-century. They continued to look back to Augsburg for inspiration and for a model for their own confession of faith. They basked in joy and confidence as they reflected on the Augsburg event.

Georg Spalatin (1484–1545), Luther's long-time friend, the former personal secretary to Elector Frederick the Wise, then a pastor in Altenburg, displayed an enthusiasm typical of those who had participated in the diet. A decade after he had served in the party of Elector John of Saxony at the diet, Spalatin prepared a history of the Reformation. With an exaggerated appraisal characteristic of 16th-century Lutheran assessments, he called the Augsburg Confession

> the most significant act that has ever taken place on earth. For on the afternoon [of the day after the festival of Saint John the Baptist] my gracious lord, the elector of Saxony [and the other princes and municipal representatives who joined him] gave public confession of their faith and of the whole Christian teaching which they permitted to be proclaimed in their princedoms, lands, and cities. They had it read in German with a fine, cheerful Christian spirit, not just in front of all the electors, princes, estates, bishops, and councillors who were present, but also in front of the Roman Imperial Majesty himself and his brother.[2]

Spalatin's exaggerated estimate of the events at Augsburg indicates how critical and significant he and his contemporaries believed the confession had been. A quarter-century later, Luther's student and biographer Johann Mathesius (1504–65), who had been studying in Wittenberg at the time of the Confession, reiterated Spalatin's view. He compared the Evangelical confession at Augsburg to a brass festival concert: "A more significant and important act, a more precious and glorious confession, has not been performed since the time of the Apostles."[3] A generation later, David Chytraeus (1531–1600), Melanchthon's devoted disciple, echoed Mathesius' judgment, placing the Augsburg Confession in the lineage of the creeds of the ancient councils and the writings of the patristic fathers.[4] In lecturing to his students at the Strassburg Academy, Johannes Pappus (1549–1610) agreed that

> the worth and excellence of this confession is such that it can rightly and deservedly be compared with the chief creeds of the orthodox church. For nothing concerning the Christian religion can be correctly expressed or conceived which does not have its basis in this confession, drawn as it is from the pure Word of God and corroborated with its most certain and clear testimonies.[5]

Chytraeus had published his *History of the Augsburg Confession* in 1576, and when fellow Wittenberg graduate Georg Coelestin (1523–79) published a similar work in 1577, Chytraeus protested that Coelestin had plagiarized Chytraeus' work. But the two agreed on the significance of the Augsburg Confession. Coelestin wrote,

> That diet was governed by divine providence, not by human counsel. For if the most excellent and gentle emperor had done everything which the papists nefariously directed him to do and had governed his actions according to their savage, monstrous—may I say diabolical—counsel, certainly the articles of our confession would not have been publicly read and heard, nor would the teaching comprehended in them have been spread and propagated in all lands and nations. Nor would we have escaped danger and the loss of life, body, and all our possessions at the diet.

Coelestin continued with a paraphrase of the oft-cited passage from Luther:

> Even Dr. Luther, as he carefully considered the events of this diet and thought about them through and through, expressed himself in these words: "The diet of Augsburg is worthy of all praise. For there the Word was presented, contrary to the expectation of all, even of the emperor himself. No one should regret what took place there. For since the papacy arose, the proper understanding of the faith has never been so well proclaimed."[6]

Johann Wigand (1523–87), another student of Luther and Melanchthon and a leading Prussian churchman of his time, briefly recounted the blossoming of the Gospel under Luther, the opposition it aroused, and the martyrdom which resulted from that op-position. He suggested that the confession at Augsburg was the natural outgrowth of this historical development.[7] Ludwig Helm-bold, a pastor and later a superintendent in Mühlhausen, who was crowned poet laureate in 1566 and whose poetry earned him the epithet "the German Asaph," found the Augsburg Confession worthy of paraphrase in verse.[8] In short, 16th-century German Lutheran commentators viewed the confession at Augsburg as a key point in both the development of Luther's Reformation and the history of the entire church.

Defining the Confession

At the same time, the commentators did not agree precisely on the definition of "the Augsburg Confession." A study of their use of the term reveals their shifting perspective of that great event that was—to use Mathesius' word cited above—"performed" at Augsburg. Three different—though certainly not mutually exclusive—defini-tions of *confession* appear in the historical analyses of Augsburg following the event. At first, *Augsburg Confession* was defined as the *act* of confessing, i.e., the verbal witness before the emperor rendered by the Evangelical princes and municipal delegates. Later, *Augsburg Confession* was equated with the *teaching* of the theo-logians and pastors of the Evangelical lands. Finally, Lutheran com-mentators viewed the *Augsburg Confession* as the *document* which the Evangelical leaders read to the diet and which set forth the teaching of the churches in their lands.

Defining Augsburg as the Act of Confessing

According to Melanchthon's good friend Friedrich Myconius (1490–1546), the ecclesiastical superintendent in Gotha, the actual *con-fessing* began in the negotiations between the Evangelical princes and Emperor Charles V in May and early June. Myconius claimed that during the course of those negotiations, the princes stated that they would rather let their heads be cut off than deny their faith. (This statement actually was made by Margrave Georg of Branden-burg-Ansbach, but Myconius attributed it to all the Lutheran princes.) Later, Philip Melanchthon set down the teaching supported by these princes in a formal schema, and the Evangelical confessors presented it to the emperor and the empire. But the confession did not stop there, according to Myconius. It continued through the subsequent negotiations between Evangelical and Roman Catholic theologians and government representatives into the autumn of 1530.[9] Mathesius also could define *Augsburg Confession* as the action of the princes in offering "a good and proper account and the basis of their faith and hope in the fear of God and good conscience, with gentleness and modesty."[10] Wigand compared the princes to John the Baptist, who also obeyed God and gave witness before the people.[11]

Defining Augsburg as the Body of Teaching

Augsburg Confession also embraced the teaching, the content conveyed by the confessors. In his biography of Luther, Mathesius states that the Elector John and his colleagues took counsel with their advisers to place Luther's teaching before the diet so that God might be honored and the elector might give witness to his faith.[12] "Whoever seeks the pure teaching of the Gospel," according to Wigand, "is led to the Augsburg Confession, for in it is comprehended not a new teaching, but the old teaching; not human teaching, but divine teaching, handed down in the records of the prophets and the apostles." Wigand concluded that the Augsburg Confession is "a confession of the teaching concerning the principal articles of faith clearly drawn from the Word of God." The confession's *materia,* the substance of which it was composed, is "spiritual matters," that is, the most significant chapters of heavenly teaching, gathered and selected from the Word of God.

Concerning the *efficient* cause, which gave the Confession its power, Wigand wrote,

> The efficient cause of the Augsburg Confession is God, although His causative power is mediate, not direct. For the Augsburg Confession is the Word of God since it is drawn out of the Word; and since this true Confession confesses the true divine name, and is not a work of human powers but of God's generous giving the light of His doctrine and the courage and zeal for confession, therefore this good work may be ascribed to Him.[13]

Wigand believed that the men who expressed their theology in the Augsburg Confession had been chosen for this task by God. God had called, illumined, equipped, and guided them in their work. These men included Luther, Melanchthon, Justus Jonas (their Wittenberg colleague), Erhard Schnepf (a follower who had worked largely in Hesse and Württemberg), Johann Brenz (the most influential South German reformer), Johann Agricola (a Wittenberg student), Georg Spalatin, and others.

Wigand understood the Confession as an expression of God's revelation and a proper, correct, and certain rule for teaching the Gospel because it flowed directly from God's Word.[14]

Defining Augsburg as Document

Wigand also recognized that *Augsburg Confession* continued to be a historical act of great significance and an influential expression of Luther's teaching because it was a document. As such, it was capable of conveying the content and the spirit of the act of confession at Augsburg to later generations. The dedication of his *History of the Augsburg Confession* to Erhard von Kunheim, a ducal councillor, began with thanks to God for those blessings He had given to Germany in "this last age of the earth." Among those blessings, Wigand listed the revival of knowledge of the ancient languages and of the liberal arts, which contain human and divine wisdom.

As a student of Luther and Melanchthon, Wigand had come to appreciate the blessing of knowledge about the creation as well as the Creator. Wigand also considered printing to be a blessing. The invention of printing enabled the church to proclaim God's Word more powerfully than at any time since the apostolic age. Wigand maintained that the Augsburg Confession in print was especially important for this proclamation.[15] In an edition of the text of the 1530 Confession, published in 1576, Wigand explained its importance. Indeed, in the battle between God's truth and the devil's lies, the

> revealed and confirmed Word of God is alone the norm for teaching and believing in God's whole church. It is the standard of judgment according to which all teachings and teachers in the entire world are to be tested, judged, and evaluated.

Nonetheless, Wigand held that, in times of controversy, the church has pledged itself to certain confessions alongside Holy Scripture. These confessions may only be taken from the Word of God, the Scriptures, and must never be exalted over Scripture or placed on its level. But the church does affirm such confessions that flow from God's Word. The three ancient creeds are examples of such confessions.[16]

Nikolaus Selnecker (1528/30–92) was a Saxon theologian who had opposed Wigand and his colleagues in the intra-Lutheran disputes of the 1550s and 1560s. He later served with Chytraeus on the team that constructed the *Formula of Concord* in 1576–77. Selnecker composed his *Historical Oration on the Life of Martin Luther* in part to reject a bias against Melanchthon among the "Gnesio-Lutheran" party to which Wigand belonged. But Selnecker shared Wigand's understanding of the Augsburg Confession. Selnecker wrote that the princes and councillors at Augsburg wanted a document composed to treat all of Christian teaching in a series of chapters. The princes boldly faced the danger of subscribing to such a document as it was read before the diet. Their confession affirmed the teaching of the Gospel that God had revived through Luther.

The forthright presentation of the Gospel made Selnecker, like Luther, recall the words of the psalmist, "I give witness before kings and am not ashamed" (Ps. 119:46). Luther's heirs were accustomed to fitting the events of their time into a Biblical context, and this included the events at Augsburg in 1530. Selnecker was confident that the confession of the princes in document form would remain until the last day. The power of this confession had already been demonstrated by the blood of holy martyrs. Selnecker cited Luther's remarks in regard to the Augsburg Confession: the more God's Word is persecuted, the more it flourishes and grows.[17] The eschatological framework of the events of Augsburg was quite clear to Selnecker and his contemporaries.

Like Wigand and Selnecker, others who published studies of the Augsburg Confession in the 1570s recognized it, above all, as a document, but they too viewed this document as the embodiment of both a courageous act of Christian testimony and the sum of Biblical teaching.

The Impact of the Confession

Georg Coelestin's four-volume work began with his evaluation of the significance of the confession. The confession proclaimed the Gospel that Luther had revived, and the trumpet call heralding the last judgment sounded through it. Coelestin dedicated his second volume to the Evangelical leaders of the empire. He recalled how God had enabled representatives of an earlier generation of princes and municipal leaders to stand before the emperor and testify to Luther's teaching of the truth. They had done so in a confession composed by Philip Melanchthon. That document's summary of Christian teaching was arranged into specific topics[18] and was expressed with remarkable clarity and sensitivity in proper order and form, without ambiguity, according to Coelestin.

Coelestin's rehearsal of the events of June 25, 1530 stressed that the Lutheran princes delivered to the diet a statement drawn from the testimonies of the prophetic and apostolic Scriptures. Coelestin, like others, emphasized the precise and lucid manner in which the Saxon councillor Christian Beyer read the confession before the diet. The effect of the confession spread far beyond the halls in which the diet met and the crowd that could hear Beyer, for Charles had the confession translated into Spanish and Italian. Several Evangelical commentators delighted in telling that the pope could not understand Latin well enough to digest their confession in that language, so he had an Italian translation prepared.

Other translations were produced for the legates of the kings of France, England, and Portugal, and for the dukes of Lorraine and Jülich. Coelestin concluded that "the Saxon Confession was disseminated through almost all the world, spreading the Gospel widely among many peoples."[19] Coelestin's exuberance may have led him to exaggerate the Confession's impact, but it reflects his understanding of the significance of what was done and said at Augsburg in 1530.

Many shared Coelestin's understanding, including David Chytraeus, who competed against Coelestin for the attention of those interested in the religious developments at the imperial diet in 1530. Chytraeus had undoubtedly become fascinated with the Augsburg Confession as a young student in Wittenberg when he lived and dined in Melanchthon's home during part of the 1540s. He went on to become a skilled historian as well as an exegete and systematic theologian at the University of Rostock. Chytraeus worked for some years to prepare his *History of the Augsburg Confession*. In the preface, he explained why he thought it necessary to write his history. First, the Augsburg Confession had become a general creed [symbol] or confession for the Lutheran churches. Second, the confrontation at Augsburg had been instrumental in transforming the Western church.

Chytraeus borrowed Spalatin's words to describe the dramatic public testimony of faith made in Augsburg on June 25, 1530. The confession was, in Chytraeus' mind, a document; but for him it was also a document which delivered the powerful impact of the Gospel itself. Chytraeus, among others, took pleasure in the ironic way in which the Gospel had been proclaimed in Augsburg. Soon after his arrival in the city, Emperor Charles had forbidden all preaching in Augsburg for the duration of the diet. Although Roman Catholic preachers did not observe this prohibition, the Evangelical preachers did. What delighted Chytraeus was the fact that 10 preachers could not have preached more effectively than did this written confession:

> Is that not splendidly clever, a great joke, that Master Eisleben [a Saxon court preacher] and the others had to keep silent, but in their place the elector of Saxony and the other princes and lords stepped forward with their written confession and preached freely in front of the imperial majesty and the entire empire, right under their noses so that they had to listen to it and could say nothing against it. . . . Christ just would not be silent at that diet and, even if they were raving mad, they had to hear more from this confession than they would have heard from an entire year of sermons. It happens as Saint Paul says: God's Word just will remain unbound. If it is forbidden in the pulpit, it has to be heard in the palaces. If the poor preachers dare not speak, then the great lords and princes speak. Finally, if all become silent, the stones will cry out, as Christ himself said.[20]

Like all his Lutheran contemporaries, Chytraeus could not think of the written Augsburg Confession without thinking of the bold proclamation of the Gospel that occurred when it was first read.

The Confession Becomes Normative for Teaching

Chytraeus' colleagues, Jakob Andreae (1528–90) and Martin Chemnitz (1522–86), had the Augsburg Confession in mind as they drafted the preface of *The Book of Concord* in autumn 1578. They stressed that the immediate background of the confession was the conflict between the Gospel and the "papistic superstition." They affirmed that the confession did no more than convey the message of the "divine, prophetic, and apostolic Scriptures."

This judgment was shared by all the Lutheran commentators of the period. For example, Wigand stated that the teaching of the Augsburg Confession would last into eternity, "for it embraces the Word of God, and the Word of God, at hand in the Holy Scriptures, remains forever." Later he told his hearers, "The foundations of this confession of God's Word [are] comprehended in the works of the prophets and the apostles. [The confessors] wished to teach or assert or proclaim nothing in the church than that which is based on the holy writings."[21]

Selnecker responded to Reformed critics by reaffirming this point of view. Antagonists had argued that a particular confession should not be used as a standard for judging what is true or false, orthodox or heretical, or what is to be taught or condemned. While Selnecker agreed that Scripture alone had the authority to be the rule and norm for teaching and faith, he insisted that there was nothing in the confessions of the Lutheran church which was not drawn purely from God's Word.[22] Selnecker believed that a document composed by Luther or Melanchthon therefore could also be authoritative. He believed that even though they were miserable sinners, the Holy Spirit had used them to revive and teach the message of Christ.[23] Luther's concept of the living voice of the Gospel and the power it conveys undergirded Selnecker's understanding of the Augsburg Confession and the other Lutheran confessional documents.

According to the preface to *The Book of Concord,* the Word of Christ had been addressed not just to the German Empire, but to "all of Christendom throughout the wide world." In the preface, Andreae and Chemnitz focused on the nature of the Augsburg Confession as a document because it had become "the contemporary symbol of the faith [of many churches and schools] in the chief articles in controversy over against both the papacy and all sorts of factions." It could serve that function because it conveyed the content and power of Scripture.

Therefore, Andreae and Chemnitz considered it their personal confession as well:

> By the help of God's grace, we, too, intend to persist in this confession until our blessed end and to appear before the judgment seat of our Lord Jesus Christ with joyful and fearless hearts and consciences.[24]

This comment indicates that they were fully aware of the eschatological significance both of the Augsburg Confession and their own confession of faith in the Formula of Concord. The sense that Christ might return at any moment, present in early days of the Reformation, had receded. Nonetheless, Chemnitz and Andreae were convinced that all of human history stands immediately before God's judgment throne. They believed that their confession was part of the life to which God had called them, a life which was moving toward their own appearance before Him.

Their comments reflect their understanding of the development of the definition of *Augsburg Confession* from the *action* of believers who boldly confronted their culture with the Word of God, through the *content* of that confession, to the *document* which was both the basis for the action and the content of the message.

The Confession as a Tool for Relationships with Other Christians

For these later 16th-century Lutherans, the confession at Augsburg continued to serve as a model. The commentary of Johann Mathesius emphasizes two characteristics of the Augsburg Confession that he says should apply to every confession of the faith. First, it must reject false teaching that deceives and leads astray; and, second, it must seek the unity and harmony of Christ's church. It must be noted that in part the condemnations of the Augsburg Confession were ecumenical devices as well as doctrinal positions. The clear rejection of sacramentarian and Anabaptist views was an essential part of the Evangelical claim to be catholic. Without such clarifying condemnations no rapprochement with the Roman Catholic party would have been possible.

The confessors at Augsburg had practiced condemnation of false teaching which would prevent true Christian unity even as they pursued that unity. Commentators on the Confession recalled attempts to force the Lutherans at Augsburg on the defensive, and they noted the Lutheran response.

Mathesius insisted that it was necessary to confront and condemn false doctrine: "the steadfast confessors and representatives of the truth of Jesus Christ" defended the Gospel also by "refuting the antichristian teaching which is full of lies, heresy, idolatry, death, and bloodshed."[25] Wigand agreed that

> divine truth cannot be conveyed unimpaired unless that which is false is refuted.... For where God reigns, the devil's rule must collapse. Where Christ takes up dwelling, the devil, brave as he may be, is forced to leave the house.[26]

The earliest reports of the confrontation at Augsburg describe it in classical Christian terms as a conflict between God and Satan, good and evil, and truth and falsehood. Myconius emphasized the villainy of "[John] Eck and other Sophists," and he accused them of being cowards and liars because they refused to permit the Confutation to be read by Melanchthon and his colleagues.[27] Spalatin depicted Duke Georg of Saxony and the other Roman sympathizers as evil plotters who went out to meet Charles V at Innsbruck to devise a way of attacking "poor Christ and His dear Word." He also depicted the Roman Catholics as theologically incompetent and dependent on threats of force, deception, and misrepresentation of the Lutheran position. Spalatin recorded the warning of Elector Joachim of Brandenburg that he would spend possessions and blood, body and life, and lands with their people to root out the Lutherans.[28]

These themes were repeated throughout the next half-century by others, including Nikolaus Selnecker. Selnecker compared Philip Melanchthon to Jonah and Daniel, saying that Melanchthon had marched unafraid into the lions' den, confronted the claws of the devil as the papal legate Campeggio thundered and flashed bolts of lightning. Melanchthon had simply responded that he could not abandon the truth. The image of the ancient martyrs lay behind

Selnecker's description. In reaction to Campeggio's storming,

> Saint Philip [Melanchthon] stood as if in the midst of lions, wolves, and bears which could tear him into little bits and pieces, but he had a superabundance of splendid courage in his slight frame, and he answered boldly, "We commit ourselves and our cause to God, our Lord."[29]

Selnecker emphasized how dire the threat to the Evangelicals had been by quoting an anonymous Roman Catholic prince:

> The Lutherans have submitted a confession written with ink. If I were emperor, I would love to give them a confutation written with rubrics, that is, one which would be in their blood.[30]

These commentators looked upon the confession at Augsburg as having been made in the same manner as the confessions of the early Christian martyrs.

Subsequent events demonstrated how accurate their assessment was. The emperor took seriously his edict of 1521 in which he set in motion the machinery to eradicate Luther's teaching and followers.[31] Those Lutherans who recounted the confession at Augsburg wanted to make clear to later generations the seriousness of the situation and the courage of their fathers in the faith. Furthermore, as Hans-Werner Gensichen has shown,[32] it was obvious to 16th-century Lutherans that it was necessary to clarify the confession by condemning the beliefs of God's enemies and the world. These commentators wanted their readers to understand this necessity and to realize that opposing falsehood was a dangerous business, one requiring them to live under the cross.

Mathesius had also observed that the confessors at Augsburg were seeking the peace and unity of the church. They were willing to make concessions on issues related to external ceremonies and episcopal power without doing any harm to their consciences or the Gospel. But their Roman Catholic opponents insisted on having their way on everything, and Mathesius concluded that Christ and Belial could not be reconciled.[33] Georg Coelestin also pointed out the conciliatory stance of the Lutheran confessors. David Chytraeus shared the same opinion.[34] This generation of Lutherans took the confessors at their word when they wrote in the preface to the Confession that we on our part shall not omit doing anything in so far as God and conscience allow that may serve the cause of Christian unity.[35]

Though the prospects for reconciliation with Rome had dimmed completely by the time of Coelestin and Chytraeus, they knew that Christian unity had been a high priority for the confessors at Augsburg, and they conveyed deep regret that all could not agree and find harmony in the Biblical truth confessed there.

The Confessors and Their Influence on the Model

The 16th-century commentators singled out different confessors when discussing different aspects of the confession-making process. When the act of confession was important, they mentioned the princes and municipal delegates. When the content of the confession was highlighted, Luther's name appeared most often. When the composition of the document was stressed, Melanchthon was given credit.

The Confessing Princes

The courage of the confessing princes was recognized throughout the 16th century. Helmbold compared the princes to the heroes of the ancient world, Dardanus of Troy, Cadmus of Thebes, Cyrus, Alexander, and Augustus; and he described each of these princely confessors in two-line verses.[36]

Spalatin focused on the virtues of his own political overlord, Elector John of Saxony. John's obedience to the regulations for the diet set by Emperor Charles demonstrated that he was a peace-loving man. His steadfast confession of the truth manifested his conviction and courage. Spalatin contrasted the upright behavior of John and his Evangelical colleagues with the conniving and bloodthirsty baiting of the Roman Catholic princes at the diet.[37] In his chapter on the Augsburg Confession, Mathesius followed Spalatin's theme. He repeated the common saying that a prince could be saved only if he died in the crib, and he suggested that this saying had been true under the papacy. However, it was no longer true of Evangelical princes. He said that those princes who had joyously confessed their

56

faith at Augsburg had taken their places in the series of pious princes stretching from David and Hezekiah through Cyrus [!], through Constantine, Charlemagne, and Ludwig of Bavaria, and down to Elector Frederick the Wise and even Charles V. (Mathesius, like many 16th-century Lutherans, frequently—albeit naively—thought that Charles had not opposed the Augsburg Confession but had merely followed bad advice from his papal councillors. It is impossible to determine whether this portrayal of Charles arose because of the desire to absolve the prince, or whether it was designed to place the Augsburg Confession in a more favorable light with Habsburg princes and imperial officials.)[38]

Wigand rehearsed the threats made against Georg of Brandenburg to turn his lands over to his nephew, and the positive inducements offered to Philip of Hesse (including the return of the lands seized from his ally, Ulrich of Württemberg) by the Habsburgs some years earlier. They resisted, Wigand noted, for

> God, who in His endless mercy raises up martyrs for His truth, gave strength to their hearts through the Holy Spirit, so that they might hold fast to the truth which they acknowledged through a fearless confession, not permitting themselves to be diverted from their confession either by the fears and terrors of the damned nor the enticement of rewards. For this blessing all saints should praise and honor God.[39]

Selnecker praised Elector John's reply when John was threatened and told that he would be required to forbid Evangelical preaching in his lands. John stated "without reserve in public" that he would rather be driven from his lands than forbid the preaching of the Gospel. Selnecker, like Mathesius and others, was delighted to cite the example of Margrave Georg of Brandenburg, who exclaimed that he would rather kneel before the emperor and let his head be cut off than abandon the Gospel.[40]

The Confessing Theologians: Melanchthon and Luther

The tension between the two leading Lutheran parties after Luther's death—the Philippists and the Gnesio-Lutherans—made the question of the authorship of the Augsburg Confession even more critical.[41] Melanchthon's biographer, Joachim Camerarius, countered

57

the "vituperation" against Philip by emphasizing how the entire burden of confessing the Evangelical teaching had been placed upon his preceptor.[42] The Gnesio-Lutheran Nikolaus Gallus, by contrast, insisted that Luther was the author and authoritative interpreter of the Augsburg Confession, because Luther had argued against the changes which Melanchthon had made in the so-called *Variata* revisions of the Confession around 1540.[43] Melanchthon had played a poor Aaron to Luther's Moses, Gallus stated. Coelestin was less explicit in his criticism of Melanchthon, yet he nonetheless pointed out that Luther had had to admonish Philip to resist compromise. Wigand described the relationship in the summer of 1530 between Philip and Martin in a different manner. Melanchthon had called Luther his father and teacher, and an instrument of God. Both men, Wigand reminded his readers, had joined others in formulating the teaching of the Augsburg Confession.[44]

Others also tried to balance the responsibility for the content of the Augsburg Confession between Luther and Melanchthon. Mathesius, in his sermonic biography of Luther in the mid-1560s, endeavored to portray Luther and Melanchthon as a team working together in the composition of the Augsburg Confession.[45] Selnecker emphasized Melanchthon's courage and steadfastness in facing down the papal theologians with whom he engaged in dialog in the summer of 1530 during the negotiations before and after the presentation of the Confession. At the same time, Selnecker was convinced that Luther played an important role in the origin of the Confession because he had directed the Evangelicals in Augsburg from Coburg and had laid the groundwork for the Confession in the Schwabach Articles.[46] Chytraeus, too, remained steadfastly loyal to his preceptor during the controversies swirling around Melanchthon in the 1560s and 1570s. Nonetheless, he stressed that Melanchthon had used Luther's words and phrases from the Schwabach Articles. He described the relationship between Luther and Melanchthon in this way in the preface to the Latin edition of his *History of the Augsburg Confession*:

> These two instruments of God, both of great benefit to the church, were endowed with different natures and gifts but shared one and the same program and goal, the glory of God and the welfare of the church, with the same urgency and a remarkable spirit. If Luther seems more vehement against Erasmus and others, a phy-

sician for the ills of the church who has a harsh touch, and Philip on the other hand seems milder and gentler, nevertheless they are equally endowed in piety, teaching, sharpness of mind, propriety of judgment, and skill at interpreting Christian teaching in controversies. Together they have proclaimed the Gospel with minds joined and with common efforts, cleansing that teaching from the darkness and errors of an earlier age, in a most faithful and felicitous fashion.[47]

In summary, the heirs of the Wittenberg leaders admired the princes as heroic civic leaders who risked land and life by standing up for the Gospel in the face of imperial wrath. At the same time they recognized that the courageous confession of the princes was made possible by the knowledge, insight, and courage of the theologians who taught the Gospel to these princes. Lutherans in the 16th century admired and respected both princes and theologians alike. Indeed, they wanted the model to stand for their successors.

Internal Controversy over the Confession

Wigand's narrative of the Augsburg Confession, delivered to the students of the University of Königsberg, was designed to move them to embrace the Confession with their whole hearts and to reject all false opinions that might militate against it.[48]

Wigand closed his narrative with the continuing history of confession in the midst of this turmoil. First, he dealt with works written in the 1530s and 1540s, such as the Smalcald Articles, which Luther had prepared for testimony at the council called by the pope and appointed for Mantua in 1537. He also analyzed the colloquies at which Lutheran negotiators had had opportunities to confess to their counterparts from the Roman camp, such as at the colloquies held at Regensburg in 1541 and 1546. Then Wigand went on to describe the turbulent times inaugurated by the military defeat of the Evangelical princes in the Smalcald War and by the emperor's attempt to reimpose Roman Catholicism upon Evangelical lands through the so-called Augsburg Interim of 1548. The unfolding of those events created a new situation that called for further confession.

The Challenge from within the Ranks

The Evangelicals were first threatened with the eradication of their movement by the Roman Catholics. The second challenge came from fellow Lutherans who, from the standpoint of Wigand and his Gnesio-Lutheran party, were unnecessarily compromising their faith for the sake of temporal peace.[49] Every age, these Lutheran confessors believed, is an age wherein confession of the faith is necessary—although certainly authoritative documents of confession will not be produced in each age. They were not surprised that threats to the integrity of their confession of the faith arose from within their own ranks. For they believed that dissension within the church had always been one of Satan's tricks of choice.

Indeed, the roots of the disputes between the Gnesio-Lutherans and their chief opponents within Late Reformation Lutheranism, the Philippists, can be traced back to the 1530s. However, the Smalcald War and the Augsburg Interim, along with the resulting compromise forged by Melanchthon and his colleagues at Wittenberg in the so-called *Leipzig Interim,* actually opened the fierce exchanges between old friends and fellow students of Luther and Melanchthon. The Philippists generally tended to be more conservative (from the viewpoint of a medieval observer), while the Gnesio-Lutherans were more radical. The former were more open to compromise and conciliation, whereas the latter were prone to "confessional confrontation." (On these two parties, see Chapter Three.) The public controversies between the two parties, though wide-ranging and stemming from a wide variety of concerns, focused on doctrinal issues to a large extent. For example, both sides insisted on salvation by grace through faith in Christ alone, but the Gnesio-Lutherans embraced language and concepts that rejected and resisted any Philippist suggestion of a diminution of Luther's radical monergism.

Compromising the Confession?

One controversy between Philippists and Gnesio-Lutherans concerned the interpretation of the Augsburg Confession itself. This debate revolved around two different incidents: (1) Melanchthon's own alterations of the text, as early as 1540, in the so-called "altered Augsburg Confession" or *Variata,* and (2) an attempt at a diet of

Evangelical princes in 1561 to define the Confession's content so broadly that it could embrace the beliefs of Elector Frederick III of the Palatinate, who at the time was drifting rapidly into Calvinism.

Wigand's narrative of the fate of the Confession noted that the Catholic negotiator at the colloquy of Regensburg in 1541, John Eck, had called Melanchthon's attention to the fact that his alterations in the Confession's text had changed the content of the Lutheran understanding of the real presence of Christ's body and blood in the Lord's Supper. Philip had denied it, but Wigand agreed with Eck on this point. Later, others protested Melanchthon's changed wording regarding the exclusive role of the Holy Spirit in bringing unbelievers to faith, and a series of other alterations as well.[50]

The diet at Naumburg in 1561 aroused a storm of protest from Gnesio-Lutherans and others not involved in the party strife because they believed that this diet had attempted to diminish a strict adherence to the Augsburg Confession's original text. The effort to include Frederick of the Palatinate in the camp of the Augsburg Confession came to naught because some princes and theologians insisted that the original text of 1530 alone, the "unaltered Augsburg Confession," be recognized as *the* Lutheran confession. (The actual Recess document issued at the conclusion of the diet reaffirmed the text of the Confession of 1530, adding that the Variata might be regarded as an explanation of the original text.[51]) In a difficult time, Wigand believed, the Lord had preserved the Confession as the symbol of proper confessing.[52]

The Gnesio-Lutheran Responses

One of the means for preserving the original text of the Confession had been its republication by Wigand and others. During the 1560s the Philippists had issued the text of the Variata in print.[53] The Gnesio-Lutherans fought back with editions of the unaltered text. In the preface to one such edition Wigand asserted that the Augsburg Confession, as "a common confession of Christendom, particularly in Germany (although it has been adopted by certain other peoples as well)," should be available in print, especially since one man had undertaken to alter this "common confession of Christian teaching." "For this alteration did not take place with the general consent and agreement of the Christians who pledged themselves to this confession. But the confession does not belong to one man but is a common confession, a confession of the church."

Wigand went on to note that Luther had not agreed to the changes. He repeated Luther's words (which he had heard from the reformer's scribe, Georg Rörer) to Melanchthon regarding the latter's alterations of the Augsburg text: "Philip, Philip, you are not doing right when you alter the Augsburg Confession so often. It is not your book, but the church's." Wigand specifically attacked the changes Melanchthon had made in Articles 4, 5, 10, 13, 15, and 17.[54] When *The Book of Concord* was constructed in 1580, it affirmed the unaltered text of the earliest printing.

Confessing Had to Continue

In the wake of the Formula of Concord's affirmation (1577) of the authority of the Augsburg Confession for Lutheran teaching of the Scripture, another controversy broke out between the Lutherans and their Calvinist opponents within Germany. Nikolaus Selnecker was among those leading the way in defending the authority of the Augsburg Confession along lines familiar in Lutheran circles. He reiterated his belief that the Confession served as a testimony to the truth of Scripture, as a suitable norm and guide for teaching in the church, and as an authoritative statement rejecting and condemning sects and heresies.[55] But the text of the Augsburg Confession alone could not suffice to meet every threat of error and deception.

Confessing had become a way of life for Lutherans in the period after Luther's death. New situations arose. New and old issues in new contexts had to be addressed. Confessing had to continue.

3

The Situation Demands Confession: Responding to the Augsburg and Leipzig Interims

The Situation

Opponents elicit confessions of the faith. The next dramatic instance of the Lutheran confession of faith began in 1548, when Roman Catholic opposition to the spread of the Lutheran message had achieved a military triumph and seemed able to eradicate it. Worms returned—25 years too late from Charles V's perspective. Not until 1546 did the emperor find himself sufficiently free from entanglements with Spanish nobles, French kings, Turkish troops, and other enemies to devote himself to the solution of the Protestant problem. Finally he was able to put some muscle into his claim of lordship over the faith of his subjects.

In that year the emperor marshalled military forces from his Iberian and central European domains and set out to eradicate "the Lutheran pest," as he had vowed to do in the Edict of Worms of 1521. His subsequent attempt to cast all of German religious life into a somewhat refined and reformed medieval mold, under papal control, evoked bold confessions of faith from Lutheran opponents and, in the words of W. D. Hauschild, "opened the age of confessionalism."[1]

Charles V hoped to guarantee the success of his crusade against the Evangelical principalities and their faith by singling out the two most prominent princely leaders of the Lutheran movement, John Frederick, the elector of Saxony, and Philip, landgrave of Hesse, and charging them with an array of state crimes. And, indeed, the two princes had committed some of these offenses in pursuing their "protesting" program against both Charles's religious policy and the papal party in Germany.

The emperor planned ahead for the battle. He and his brother Ferdinand, king of Bohemia, struck an alliance with some other Evangelical princes who, apparently out of political expediency, thought it wiser to maintain peace with the emperor than fight for the Evangelical cause. Chief among them was Duke Moritz of Saxony, John Frederick's cousin and Philip's son-in-law.

Emperor Charles V, based in Austria, marched with his forces into southern Germany in the summer of 1546. Evangelical armies under John Frederick and Philip might have withstood the attack, but after only a couple of months into the war, Moritz's forces invaded John Frederick's lands. So the two Evangelical princes led their troops back to Saxony, cleared Moritz's occupation forces out of John Frederick's territory, and awaited the northward advance of the emperor's army in the spring of 1547.

On April 24, 1547, a field urchin showed the imperial troops where to ford the Elbe in order to surprise the Evangelical armies encamped near Mühlberg. On that day Charles took Philip and John Frederick prisoner, condemned them to death, and presumed that he was indeed lord of the religious policy and the religious destiny of Germany.

Charles did not execute Philip and John Frederick. Instead, he kept them jailed for several years because they stubbornly and scornfully rejected his efforts to convert them to the new imperial program for "recatholicization." The princes lost their lands temporarily (John Frederick's family never regained all its territory) and their health, but they were heralded as confessors of the faith. Particularly the imprisonment of John Frederick elicited a number of popular ballads and songs. Some of these regarded the elector as a "martyr" and a "confessor of the faith."[2] By refusing to accept Charles's compromise in the Interims, he and Philip did model that spirit of confessing the faith that both had exhibited at Augsburg in 1530.

The Augsburg Interim

Charles V was determined to restore unity of faith under his own rule to his German empire. With his brother Ferdinand at his side, he convened what was called "the armored diet" at Augsburg in the fall of 1547. Among this diet's tasks was the regularizing of German religious life. Charles appointed a commission of theologians to formulate a program of reform. On this commission, among others, sat two "Erasmian, politique"[3] Roman clergy (Julius von Pflug and Michael Helding), one renegade Evangelical (Johann Agricola, court preacher in Berlin), one of Charles's Spanish theologians (Domingo de Soto), and Ferdinand's court preacher (Pedro Malvenda). This core group worked out a *Formula for Reformation,* which Charles published on May 15, 1548, as the religious law of the land in all Evangelical territories under his rule.[4] He may or may not have intended to extend this policy to all his lands—scholars have debated this issue;[5] but in fact the Roman Catholic estates of the empire insisted on limiting it to Evangelical principalities.

This *Formula for Reformation* became popularly known as the *Augsburg Interim* because Charles designed it as an interim policy, to last only until the council which had begun to meet at Trent would conclude its restructuring of Western Christendom. The Erasmian inclinations of the Interim's chief authors appear in its program, to be sure; but fundamentally this document called for the restoration of medieval beliefs and practices, cleansed of what its authors believed to be superstition. Its treatment of justification through faith recognized the prevenient role of God's grace, but it emphasized that justification occurs through both the faith and the love of the individual. Thus, it contradicted the heart of the message that Luther identified in the Scriptures, the assurance of salvation on the basis of God's promise—the promise that because justification has already taken place through Christ's redemptive act, the believer is saved through faith. According to Charles's *Formula* the evaluation of the human creature's works still stands at the center of justification. The Interim document also taught that in the mass the church continues the sacrifice of Christ on the cross. Thus, it directly countered Luther's objections to the use of the Lord's Supper as a human means of contributing to and participating in the process of salvation.

In addition to addressing fundamental doctrinal issues, the Augsburg Interim sought to regulate the worship life and the organization of Evangelical churches. These mandates for liturgy and polity were, as Hans Christoph von Hase observed, an "innovative and truly significant . . . attack on the Gospel."[6] In connection with the celebration of the mass, the conduct of the seven sacraments, the observation of processions and festivals, the use of indulgences and vestments, and the veneration of the saints, the Augsburg Interim demanded that the churches in Evangelical lands abandon "innovations" and return to a way of life close to that practiced before Luther called for reform. Charles's reform program also prescribed a return to the discipline and administration of the bishops loyal to Rome, which meant in turn the suppression of all Evangelical teaching and practice. Finally, the Augsburg Interim proscribed every attempt to criticize it or the Roman church; it forbade the preaching or publication of Evangelical ideas.

Efforts to Enforce the Augsburg Interim

The emperor began the enforcement of his new religious policy in the summer of 1548. Wherever in south and central Germany he exercised power, Charles strove to introduce the Augsburg Interim. Some princes and city councils (such as those of Strassburg and Nuremberg) worked out compromises through negotiation.[7] Some lands and cities were occupied by imperial troops. However, with but one exception, no Evangelical pastor or theologian of any stature accepted the Interim. Caspar Huberinus (1500–1553) had helped establish the Lutheran faith in Augsburg over two decades, before accepting a call to Oehringen in 1544. He was persuaded by his brother-in-law, Georg Sigismund Seld, vice-chancellor in Charles V's government, to support the Interim. Hundreds were forced to flee their pulpits—which often remained empty because the emperor and his Roman supporters did not have sufficient personnel to replace them.

While the enforcement of the Interim may have eliminated the Evangelical leadership at the local level, the emperor could not mount a successful counter-reforming force, at least not immediately. By the time sufficient personnel had been developed in Germany, events had moved far beyond the persecution employed to impose the Augsburg Interim. The Protestant princes had won legality for their Augsburg Confession through the Religious Peace of Augsburg of 1555, and it had again become the norm for religious life in most of the areas that Charles had tried unsuccessfully to return to the old religion.

Resistance in Northern Germany

In northern Germany Charles's power had seemed even less persuasive all along. Some princes supported him, for instance, Johann Agricola's protector, Elector Joachim of Brandenburg. But other governments, such as that of John Frederick's sons in Thuringia and those of a number of Hanseatic cities, ignored Charles's directive to implement the Interim.

Particularly hard pressed by the unfolding developments of the diet of Augsburg (of late 1547 and early 1548) was Moritz of Saxony. His reward for taking sides against his relatives and fellow religionists on the field of battle had been the title of elector of Saxony and the electoral Saxon lands, both of which had belonged to his cousin, John Frederick. Moritz thought that he had secured the promise of Charles and Ferdinand that he would not have to institute changes in the religious life of Saxony, in exchange for opposing Philip and John Frederick in the war. Charles and Ferdinand conveniently could not recall such oral assurances, and they demanded that Moritz return Saxony to the Roman obedience through the observance of the Augsburg Interim.

Resistance at Wittenberg

Moritz had not only been awarded the office of imperial elector and the lands which went with it, but he also laid claim to the University of Wittenberg located in those lands and its theological faculty. Although the faculty had strongly supported John Frederick's campaign against the emperor with a number of tracts justifying such armed resistance to his overlord, its members now felt obliged to support the new prince whom God had given them, namely, Moritz. As the new elector's advisers, Melanchthon and his colleagues came to feel the pressures which the situation imposed upon their prince: pressures on the one side from the emperor, who was determined to bring his German lands into unity under the Roman obedience, and on the other side from nobles and peasants and their own consciences—all of them insisting on faithfulness to the Gospel that Luther had preached.

Melanchthon and his colleagues recognized that "accepting this book [the Augsburg Interim] would amount to admitting that our churches have taught falsely up to this point and have caused wanton schism."[8] That admission Melanchthon could not make. He wrote that although peace must be ardently pursued, "the solemn command not to deny nor to persecute the clear teaching of the truth of the Gospel compels us to the confession of the correct teaching which is being proclaimed in our churches."[9] Melanchthon also found much that was objectionable in the specifics of the Interim's doctrine and its prescriptions for practice.[10] However, he believed that God had given the prince jurisdiction over the lives of his people, also over their religious lives, and he believed that it was his duty to serve his prince unless such service clearly departed from the Word of God. Furthermore, Melanchthon was concerned for peace both in the church and in the empire. He feared that Moritz's active resistance to Emperor Charles and King Ferdinand could bring Spanish occupation forces into the north and result in hundreds more Lutheran pulpits being emptied by papal and imperial persecution.

Moritz's secular councillors were more concerned with secular peace than with religious truth, but together the new elector's secular and spiritual advisors wrestled with the political problem of staving off the emperor while preserving as much of the Reformation as possible. This was not to be a simple task. Julius von Pflug and Michael Helding had both become bishops in Saxony and were part of the emperor's means of keeping watch over his uncertain ally there. Thus, in a series of meetings during the summer and autumn of 1548, the various groups that constituted Moritz's circle of advisors hammered out a compromise which would, they hoped, teach Lutheran doctrine and project an image of conformity with the imperial religious policy at the same time.

In order to accomplish this, Melanchthon embraced the ancient Stoic concept of *adiaphora,* indifferent things, which are in and of themselves neither good nor evil, neither commanded nor prohibited, but which may be used for good or ill in different circum-

68

stances. Already at Augsburg, Melanchthon found this concept a useful tool in trying to come to agreement with his Roman opponents. Luther, however, had expressed his deep misgivings about such an approach, even though he eventually was willing to grant that concessions in this realm might be made.[11]

The Leipzig Interim: An Attempt at Compromise

Through long negotiations Moritz's government finally managed to forge a compromise, which it presented to the Saxon estates in December 1548, and which it introduced only haphazardly and partially into its domains. This compromise was promptly dubbed the *Leipzig Interim* by other members of the Wittenberg movement who rejected any attempt to compromise with the pope and emperor. The Leipzig Interim was indeed supposed to explain clearly and defend forcefully the Lutheran understanding of justification through faith. Instead it proposed a mixture of faith and works, of God's grace and human love, which pleased no one and muddled the fundamental concern of the Lutherans beyond recognition. Its use of the concept of adiaphora resulted in a treatment of Baptism, the Lord's Supper, confession and absolution, confirmation, marriage, ordination, and extreme unction as similar rites, even though it did not specifically label them sacraments. It restored much of the practice of the canon of the mass, and it affirmed the use of many medieval customs and rites, such as certain Marian holidays and other festivals, among them Corpus Christi; abstinence from meat on Fridays, Saturdays and other fast days; and the use of certain vestments and the monastic canonical hours. Finally, it also recognized the power of papally appointed bishops over Evangelical churches, without suggesting effective limits upon this power.[12]

Some Evangelicals had already addressed the crisis caused by the Interims by turning to confession and confrontation rather than compromise. Martin Bucer and Paul Fagius had been driven from Strassburg into exile in England because of their objections to the Augsburg Interim. Johann Brenz was driven from Schwäbisch Hall into hiding somewhere in Württemberg as the Interim was enforced.[13] They are but prominent examples of the several hundred pastors who were driven from office by the imperial Interim.

In the north, beyond the grasp of Charles's occupation army, voices of defiant protest had been raised from a number of places. Out of their protest and the rejoinders and recriminations that Moritz's theologians shot back in return, a division arose within the Wittenberg movement.

Confrontation versus Compromise

Two parties developed out of the differences among Luther's followers on how best to respond to the Augsburg Interim. Since the late 18th century, scholars have labeled as *Philippists* those who followed Melanchthon in supporting Moritz's policy of compromise, and those who opposed that policy were called *Gnesio-Lutherans.* Members of both parties claimed and wanted to be Luther's faithful followers. In one way or another almost all of them also demonstrated the influence of Melanchthon. But they were divided by differing approaches to a number of issues regarding the teaching and life of the Lutheran church.

The differences between the two parties may be treated under at least four broad categories. In each, the Philippists appear to be more conservative (from a late medieval perspective); and the Gnesio-Lutherans seem more radical in their expression of Luther's message.

(1) Out of the controversies over the Interims grew several doctrinal disputes. In each of them a more radical view of sin and grace was defended by the Gnesio-Lutherans, while the Philippists tended to express their opinions with something more of a traditional flavor.

(2) The Gnesio-Lutherans rejected more of the medieval liturgical heritage than did the Philippists; and they were far more zealous in condemning the medieval system of church government, the papacy, which both parties regarded as the "Antichrist."

(3) The Philippists strove to accommodate themselves to the policies of their rulers and believed that the state should exercise some power over the church. The Gnesio-Lutherans sharply rejected any secular government's claim to power within the church and often sharply criticized their rulers for a variety of sins.

(4) Finally, the Philippists sought peace within the church, and on occasion they chose silence over public expression of their views in order to preserve it. The Gnesio-Lutherans believed in bold and

confrontational confession of the faith.[14] This stance was intensified by a heightened eschatological awareness. They firmly believed that the Last Day was at hand.

The Interims Confronted in the North: The Gnesio-Lutheran Confessors

Nikolaus von Amsdorf

Nikolaus von Amsdorf (1483–1565), the grandfather of the Gnesio-Lutheran party and Luther's friend since the early 1510s, was ousted from his post as the Evangelical bishop of Naumburg-Zeitz by the Smalcald War (1546) and was replaced by the Roman Catholic theologian and Saxon nobleman Julius von Pflug. Amsdorf made his way back to Magdeburg, where he had introduced the Reformation twenty years earlier. Returning to the city in 1548, he joined a group which would become the nucleus of the Gnesio-Lutheran movement. From Magdeburg he issued his confession of faith entitled *Answer, Creed, and Confession on the Wonderful and Winsome Interim* (1548). Amsdorf took for granted that believers would make public confession of their faith, even in the face of the coercive power of the Imperial Majesty, since the Word of God had to be held firmly against all deception and persecution, especially in "these last times" in which Amsdorf believed he was living. The principle of confessing in the face of coercion was reflected also in the "memorandum," issued about the same time by Amsdorf and other theological advisors of John Frederick's sons as support for their rejection of the Augsburg Interim.[15] Two years later Amsdorf countered the Wittenberg defense of Moritz's adiaphoristic policy (of compromise previously described). Amsdorf directly attacked the electoral Saxon appeal to Luther for support of their actions. Luther never would have conceded such compromises to the Antichrist, Amsdorf wrote, but would have defied imperial commands and anything else that supported the papal denial of the Gospel.[16] For this comrade of Luther, under threat from the Interim, confrontational confession was a necessary and natural way of living as a Christian.

The Ministeria of Lübeck, Hamburg, and Lüneburg

The same point of view was shared in a number of north German cities. The ministeria of three of them—Lübeck, Hamburg, and Lüne-burg—issued their own *Confession and Declaration on the Interim* in 1548. They, too, took for granted that Christians must "attest and confess" the faith against error, such as that in the Augsburg Interim.[17] They did so, acutely aware that in this context their confession had to do both with God's truth and with the preservation of the institution of the Evangelical church. As Wolf-Dieter Hauschild has observed,

> It must be confessed that the Reformation from its very beginning was not merely an ecclesiastical undertaking. In its various phases the political dimension of theology, the way in which politics determined its course and its political consequences, is apparent. The confession of the faith was first of all intended as purely religious and yet had political implications, often unwanted. Precisely because the Lutherans occasionally underestimated this side of their confession, developments arose which damaged the Reformation not only as a political but also as a religious movement. That is clear in the attitude of the Wittenbergers toward the Interim. The theologians of the Hansa cities [the north German commercial league] were quite different in that they grasped its political dimensions from the very beginning.[18]

Joachim Westphal

Particularly sharp in his critique of the Interim was the leader of the Reformation in the Hanseatic League city of Hamburg, Joachim Westphal (1510–1574), who had studied with Luther and Melanchthon at Wittenberg. He published a series of critiques of both Interims. These critiques were based on his belief that the "saints exercise their faith in seeking external good but above all spiritual good, [that is,] the Word of God, the increase of faith and love, constancy, perseverance in confessing the truth and in worshiping God; they seek first God's kingdom and his righteousness because they know that this leads to eternal life."[19]

Westphal was soberly realistic about what such perseverance in the confession of the truth would mean for believers: because of their confession the faithful are persecuted. The story of Moses reminds believers that the confession of the faith leads them to give up fatherland, home, relatives, the courts of kings and princes, riches and other comforts of life—and that they do so with a calm spirit.[20]

Among Westphal's special concerns was the refutation of the Adiaphorists' assertion that doctrine and ceremony could be separated. He insisted that the confession to which Christ calls Christians is given also in the realm of externals, such as the form of the worship service. With pointed reference to the regulations imposed by the Interims, Westphal observed that even if it means resisting governmental authorities, believers must give confession of their faith also through such outward elements of ecclesiastical life.[21]

Matthias Flacius Illyricus

An even mightier voice than Westphal's thundered across northern Germany in the months following his first critique. It came from a foreigner, a young theologian half-Italian and half-Croatian: Matthias Flacius. His uncle, Balda Lupetino, had been murdered by Roman Catholic officials because of his adherence to Luther's ideas. As a young student Flacius himself had found in Luther's personal counsel the comfort that turned back the tide of despair engulfing him. Flacius, called Illyricus because of his national origin, in the end was called a good deal worse by Melanchthon and his defenders— and even by many of his own friends—because of his uncompromising critique of every failure to confess the Word of God boldly.

In 1544 Flacius began teaching Hebrew at the University of Wittenberg. He was a respected junior faculty member when the Augsburg Interim was published. He looked to his older colleagues on the theological faculty to provide leadership in the Lutheran rejection of its abominations. Instead, they equivocated. Flacius could not understand this attitude. In Venice his uncle had suffered imprisonment and finally lynching because he had confessed Luther's understanding of the Gospel; his preceptor, Melanchthon, who had enjoyed Luther's comradeship for a quarter century, would now rather compromise than confess. When Flacius' pleas and urgings that others publicly confess their faith against the Interim went ignored, frustration finally drove Flacius to take matters into his own hands.

He began by publishing four tracts, using the pseudonyms Johann Hermann, Joannes Waremund, Theodor Henetus, and Christian Lauterwar.[22] He edited an attack on the mass which Johann Agricola, the Evangelical participant in the composition of the Augsburg Interim, had published in 1527; and he published letters from Luther that opposed any compromise with the papacy. Only reluctantly did he move toward direct public criticism of Melanchthon and his other colleagues. But the Leipzig Interim drove him to that in the first days of 1549.[23] As a result, his situation became untenable. His colleagues were angry, and his prince, Elector Moritz, became embittered by this treasonous opposition. Flacius left Wittenberg in the spring of 1549 and after some weeks of sojourn settled in the city of Magdeburg.

Some argued that Flacius had no right to be engaging in theological discussion at all since he did not have a call to a theological faculty. Flacius countered the criticism by arguing that, first of all, he had a call to the Wittenberg faculty as an instructor in the language of the Old Testament, a call from which he had been forced but not dismissed. Furthermore, he was called to confess the faith by his baptism and by the command of God to love both God and neighbor. In a situation such as that of the Interims no Christian could be silent, he argued.[24]

Flacius and his colleagues at Magdeburg consistently opposed both silence and the concept of "amnesty," namely, forgetting the errors and mistakes of the past without addressing them forthrightly, a tactic that Melanchthon and his colleagues favored. The Wittenbergers suggested that compromise and silence might be justified with Biblical examples, including Abraham, who did not confess that Sarah was his wife (Gen. 12:11–20, 20:1–14); David, who feigned madness before King Achish (1 Sam. 21:10–16); and Christ and Paul, who answered the Pharisees very circumspectly at times. Flacius noted that none of these were situations in which the clarity and confession of God's Word were at stake.[25] Not even personal relationships should obstruct the Christian's confession of the faith, Flacius's co-worker Gallus asserted, even though he and his comrades in Magdeburg and Hamburg tried to maintain their friendship with the Philippists as the disputes over the Interims became increasingly acrimonious.[26]

Magdeburg earned the label "God's chancellery" in the period between the Augsburg Interim and the city's capitulation to imperial forces under Moritz's command in 1551. During those three years the ministerium of Magdeburg, its exiled associates—such as Flacius, and various lay supporters in the municipal government sustained the Lutheran critique of both Interims with the aid of several active printing shops. Flacius fell in with Amsdorf and a number of others, above all Nikolaus Gallus (1516–1570). Gallus was a Wittenberg graduate and exiled pastor from Regensburg on the Danube. Charles V's tentacles had reached there with sufficient power to compel the Evangelical city council of Regensburg to strike a compromise with his Interim. As a result Gallus was exiled from the city.

Confession against the Leipzig Interim began not only with Flacius's publications but also with the defiance of two pastors in the town of Torgau—Gabriel Zwilling and Michael Schultheiss. In mid-April 1549, they refused to introduce the Interim provisions into the religious life of their congregation. Moritz had Zwilling and Schultheiss deposed. But Flacius and his friends were still beyond Moritz's reach in 1549, and a torrent of tracts poured from their pens and presses.[27]

These tracts paid relatively little attention to the concept of confessing the faith; they simply presumed it. Yet one key element of the dispute with the Adiaphorists of Wittenberg—and their colleagues at the University of Leipzig—was expressed in the phrase, "nothing is indifferent in a situation that demands confession." Flacius could not understand Melanchthon's apparent willingness to "serve two masters" (Matt. 6:24). Flacius believed that the Wittenbergers' efforts at a compromise to preserve the Augsburg Confession obscured its meaning rather than made it clear. He believed that the Wittenbergers ought to recognize God's call for repentance in the persecution that was threatening them and that repentance could lead only to forthright confession of the faith. For Flacius, the church was "not wood and stone but the assembly of Christians . . . who hear God's Word and confess it," and he was firmly convinced that the church was engaged in its final struggle before Judgment Day, contending against those human and demonic powers that were attempting to snuff out God's Word and His church in the final days.[28]

The Necessity of Confessionally Confronting Compromise

At the heart of the dispute over adiaphora and the Leipzig Interim stood the disagreement over the necessity of confession against the compromise imposed by Moritz's government. Joachim Mehlhausen rightly observes, from one perspective, "In the controversy over adiaphora it finally came down to the question whether this kind of 'weakening of proper worship' [through compromise in 'adiaphora'] constituted a direct threat [to the gospel] or not."[29] Ernst Koch even more correctly observes, from another perspective, that "the essential point at issue can be determined rather exactly: it concerns differing understandings of the two-governments doctrine" [regarding the relationship of church and state and their roles and competence in deciding ecclesiastical matters].[30] The Gnesio-Lutherans saw themselves locked in a struggle over the freedom of the church to do its own God-given tasks without governmental interference. Only of secondary significance was the concern about adiaphorism as a concept or policy.

The valid observations by both Mehlhausen and Koch concerning the controversies over the two Interims and adiaphora must be understood in the light of the basic Gnesio-Lutheran conviction that the faith must be confessed publicly. In the first instance the opponents of adiaphorism insisted on confessing the faith through proper rites and usages as well as correct teaching; in the second instance they insisted on confessing the faith in defiance of the wiles of a secular government which would compromise the faith for its own purposes and compel or entice the church to go along with its compromise. Precisely from these two perspectives the people around Amsdorf, Westphal, Flacius, and Gallus, in Hamburg, Magdeburg, and other places, expressed their understanding of the role of confession of the faith in the life of the church as they were beginning to consolidate into the Gnesio-Lutheran party.

Melanchthon believed that the confession of faith concerned doctrine, the summary of Biblical teaching; he believed it must be publicly affirmed. But because he believed that the governmental authorities had a God-given role to play in the life of the church, he accepted the proposition that, though Christ alone determines what is to be taught in the church, secular rulers have the responsibility for keeping order in the church and determining how it is to be administered. He asserted that the freedom of the Christian consists only in the forgiveness of sins and that exercise of the faith in the rites and usages of the church lies under governmental jurisdiction.[31]

Against Yielding on Adiaphora

Flacius rejected Melanchthon's principle for two reasons. He rejected the concept that the secular government could govern the church (although he was enough of a 16th-century man to take it for granted that rulers are obliged to support the church—without interfering in its affairs!). Flacius also rejected Melanchthon's underlying concept that Biblical teaching could be separated from its manifestations in the worship life and administrative forms of the church. Perhaps it was the Hebrew professor in Flacius which rebeled at such a separation of the internal and external aspects of the life of the church. Whatever the reason, he refused to acknowledge that the expressions of the faith—in praise and in confession—could be divided so easily from the faith itself.

For Flacius, Gallus, Amsdorf, and their colleagues the evaluation of confession was not to be conducted in some ethereal philosophical realm—not in the professor's study—but rather in the pew, in pastoral practice, in the midst of the impact that confession has on those who need to hear it. In the case of the Interims controversies, that meant that confession must speak clearly both to papal foes and to the people of the parishes entrusted to the Lutheran confessors. The Gnesio-Lutherans believed that cultural context, perceptions, and presuppositions, not theory, determined whether the use of specific adiaphora affected the confession of faith.

"The situation demands confession," the Magdeburgers insisted as they looked at the options which the Lutherans had following the emperor's issuance of the Augsburg Interim. As they reacted to the Leipzig Interim, they again felt that the situation compelled them to confess. If they failed to confess, they believed that they would bring into jeopardy their own relationship with God and the salvation of their heirs, for only through the clearly confessed Word of God can people be saved from their sins. Both Interims, the Gnesio-Lutherans were convinced, obscured the Gospel of Christ.

In this particular situation, that Gospel was being obscured not only by false teaching but also by the actions of the leadership of the church. "Confession consists also of [the proper use of] adiaphora, for we confess and explain the faith of our heart not only with words but also with deeds and external behavior."[32] Therefore, Flacius could formulate "a general rule regarding ceremonies":

> All ceremonies and ecclesiastical usages are free in themselves, as ever. But when they are imposed through coercion, or through the erroneous impression that they are [necessary for true] worship and must be observed, or through deceit, or through pressure as a public initiation of godlessness, or when they do not edify the church of God in some way or other but disrupt it and mock God, then they are no longer adiaphora.[33]

Flacius observed that it was an adiaphoron for Daniel to pray by his window (Dan. 6:6–13), but that prayer had also become an occasion in which his confession of his faith in God was demanded. It was a matter of indifference whether the Corinthians ate meat from the sacrifice of idols; in that case Paul taught that the best confession would shield the weak of faith (1 Cor. 8:4–13). Jesus refused to observe custom and wash his hands in order to make a confession before the Pharisees regarding their regulations (Mark 7:1–9). "Therefore it is true and more than true that confession does consist in the proper use of adiaphora."[34]

Perhaps the best example of the Magdeburgers' handling of an issue of adiaphora that arose out of the Leipzig Interim is the discussion which they had with their Philippist opponents over the wearing of the surplice. Some Saxon congregations had retained the surplice when the Reformation was introduced; in others, laying it aside had been an important symbol of the rejection of the medieval papacy and the embrace of Luther's Reformation. The Gnesio-Lutherans did not object to wearing vestments. They did object to the imposition of a vestment which had once been removed to signal the adoption of the Lutheran faith. No matter how much the preacher might explain to the congregation that assuming the surplice was an indifferent matter, the congregation would understand that the preacher was bowing again to Rome and assuming the old ways which had been rejected in the village a decade or a generation earlier. Furthermore, the congregation might think that the preacher felt free to compromise in matters regarding the faith and would infer that if that could be done in one area, it could be done in others.

Gallus and Flacius addressed their opponents: You say that you still make the same oral confession. Actions and deeds also confess the faith, and they dare not be contrary to the words of confession. Your oral confession will never be sufficient to wipe away the stain of denial which has been made through that vestment. For many will know only that you put on the vestment. They will not examine carefully the specific ideas of your sermons.

The Magdeburgers dismissed the argument that the surplice was a vestment of the church, not of the pope. The perception in the congregation was all important to them, and they knew that parishioners would see the papacy's hand in the reassumption of the old garb. Furthermore, Flacius and Gallus believed that the parishioners would be right; they knew that the surplice would not be returning to some Saxon chancels if the pope were not threatening persecution.[35] They urged pastors to encourage their people to steadfastness in their faith both through their words and through example: "Under these circumstances, at this time, we cannot approve of [reassuming] the surplice. Apart from this factor and these circumstances, it is completely free, something one may do or not do."[36]

Hans Christoph von Hase summarized the concern of Flacius, which his associates shared:

> With the concept of *casus confessionis* [a situation which demands confession], he [Flacius] made it clear that witness to Christ is a living unity of correct teaching, personal confession, ecclesiastical discipline, order, and proper usages, which are unequivocal signs of the faith. All of these "build up" the faith. Correspondingly, the offense which destroys the faith also embraces more than merely the adulteration of the message through false teaching. Faith is not only adulterated but directly destroyed when deceit, compromising with opponents, insufficient discipline, scandalous usages, and papal regulations are given credibility.[37]

Such offense, according to Flacius, makes people tired of the faith, deprives them of proper support, and distresses them with innovations.[38] Therefore, confession must be made, when the situation demands, also in the use of adiaphora.

Against Yielding to Secular Government

Furthermore, confession must be made, they maintained, against the interference of those who have no call to impose their own will upon the church, even if—or especially if—they be rulers. The Gnesio-Lutheran party maintained the theories which all Lutherans had used to justify armed resistance to superior governmental authorities by lesser magistrates, even after the Philippists had abandoned those theories and signed on as Moritz's house theologians. The Gnesio-Lutherans enunciated the Wittenberg understanding of the two governments (or realms) clearly, above all in the so-called Magdeburg Confession of 1550.[39] In the decade following the Interims controversies, the Gnesio-Lutherans continued to develop this Wittenberg doctrine of the right to resist governmental authority for just cause. Alongside that doctrine they continued to assert the independence of the church from secular coercion. In line with Luther's understanding of God's assignment of callings to every *person*, they taught that God has assigned specific responsibilities to the pastors of the church and other specific responsibilities to princes and city councils. Neither may attempt to do the other's work without running afoul of God's design for human living.[40]

Against the associates of Melanchthon in Wittenberg and Leipzig, Flacius and his colleagues argued that the church owed secular rulers no obedience or cooperation which would silence or subvert the confession of the truth, as they believed the Philippists indeed were doing. No matter what the implications for the secular government, the public ministry must remain public in its confession. Pastors are called by God to teach the Word of God clearly and correctly to their people for their salvation; rulers have been given other assignments in God's world, Flacius insisted. Therefore, he believed that he and his comrades were more than justified—they were called and therefore compelled by God to confess the faith, even if that meant defying the rulers whom God had appointed to govern secular life in their lands. Flacius believed that, by trying to interfere with the church's confession, those rulers were disrupting God's design for human life that had given them control only over temporal matters, not over those concerning God's Word. Those matters are the province of the church alone.[41]

Toward Clarity through Confession

What principles divided those men who had studied together in Wittenberg and caused them to separate over the issues raised by the Interims? What factors behind the facts created two parties—the Gnesio-Lutherans and the Philippists—and led each to strive to define its positions through the collections called "bodies of teaching" (the Philippist preference) or through new confessions (the Gnesio-Lutheran choice) and thus enter the "age of confessionalism"?

The disputes over the Interims and adiaphora reveal different views of society: Melanchthon understood society to be an organic whole, working smoothly in its various parts, ecclesiastical and secular, as they cooperated—even through compromise. Flacius rejected that view and believed that the power of sin was so strong that it would continually disrupt the harmonies which God wanted to be present in human living. Melanchthon was convinced that God had called the state to share power with pastors and theologians in the church; the Magdeburgers insisted that the church be sole ruler of its own affairs, particularly its own confession. Experience led men like Amsdorf and Flacius to prize the clear confession of the faith above all else, for they had seen how easily the comfort of the Gospel could be stolen by the persecutions and pressures mounted by papal opponents. Melanchthon and his associates had less experience in facing the reality of struggles such as those which Amsdorf had undergone in Magdeburg against the archbishop's priests or which Flacius had seen in Venice, with its inquisition. Melanchthon's associates strove for temporal peace as the best guarantee of the continued preaching of the Gospel in their midst. The leaders of the Philippist party were largely professors who could be satisfied with abstract formulations; the Gnesio-Lutherans were for the most part parish pastors, who felt the implications of those formulations in the lives of the people who would be affected by them in daily life. Their pastoral sensitivity led them to defend the precious heritage which Luther had given them through bold confession of the faith.

The recriminations over actions during the Interim controversies continued to irritate and offend the disputing factions of the Wittenberg movement for a quarter century, until the Formula of

81

Concord laid matters to rest. With regard to the issue of adiaphora, it did so in its tenth article, with a decision which affirmed the Gnesio-Lutheran emphasis on the freedom of the church, even though it did not lay out carefully and clearly the full theoretical structure of the Gnesio-Lutherans' argument. But the spirit of confessing the faith exhibited at Augsburg and the consciousness of its necessity continued to inform late Reformation German Lutheranism during the controversies of the third quarter of the 16th century.

Yet differences in tone crept in. Confidence regarding the power of their message had led the Lutherans to issue a joyous shout to the world, in hopes of bringing the whole church to join in their confession. After a quarter century of rising recrimination and persecution, capped by a war and the imposition of the Interim by occupation forces, the joyous shout too often turned into a defensive yell, and the sound of hope was muted. The apocalyptic mood certainly played its part in sounding the ominous undertone. The confident hopes of bringing others to share in the confession was too often overridden by a fear that the Lutherans would lose, by sword or deceit, the precious gift of the Gospel. They had to hang onto it for dear life lest they not have it anymore to share.

The Interims Confronted in the South: Ludwig Rabus's Theology of Martyrdom

In south Germany, as mentioned above, the suppression of the Lutheran confession was more effective because of the presence of imperial troops. There, expressions of opposition and confession took different forms. Johannes Brenz, the reformer of the imperial city of Schwäbisch Hall, wrote (from hiding) against the Augsburg Interim. Flacius cited Brenz's commentary on John 11 in one of his own tracts. Brenz not only insisted on the necessity of confessing the faith but also on the connection between words and deeds in public confession. Submitting to the coercion of the papal party in the realm of ceremonies would undercut the proclamation of the Gospel just as surely as would outright false teaching. Believers must be ready to risk danger and submit to persecution if necessary to make their confession of faith clear before the world. They must rest on Christ's promise, "Everyone who confesses me before men, I also will confess before my Father who is in heaven" (Matt. 10:32).[42]

Ludwig Rabus in a Time of Martyrs

Brenz was not the only south German pastor who raised his pen against the Augsburg Interim. While he went into hiding in the southwestern German principality of Württemberg under the protection of its dukes, a former Wittenberg student named Ludwig Rabus (1524–1592) began work on a massive literary weapon to serve in the battle against the Interim. In the nearby city of Strassburg the city council worked out a compromise with Charles V regarding the Augsburg Interim. It sent two pastors, Martin Bucer and Paul Fagius, into exile and brought Roman Catholic priests, who were prepared to observe the Interim, into several of the town's parishes. One of those displaced from his pulpit by this action was Ludwig Rabus, the recently called pastor of the Münster, a church in the center of the city. In the months following his transfer from the Münster, Rabus embarked on the compilation of a massive collection of stories of Christian martyrs. He began with the ancient martyrs and subsequently added volumes, reproducing stories from the late medieval and contemporary periods.[43] In the prefaces to the eight volumes of the first edition of his martyrology (the first Protestant collection of martyr stories on this scale) and in the prefaces of the two volumes of its second edition, in 1570 and 1571, Rabus laid out a theology of confession.

Rabus believed that the Evangelical understanding of Scripture which he had learned at Wittenberg (and which now was so severely threatened both by political persecution and false teaching) was true and worthy of public confession for a number of reasons (reasons often cited in other Lutheran literature of the time as well). He believed that this teaching is "the very first and oldest teaching and has been present from the beginning," when God taught it to Adam and Eve. This teaching is pure. It brings to light things that human reason and wisdom cannot find nor comprehend, such as the Trinity, the origin and cause of sin and evil, and the justification of the sinner. This teaching, Rabus asserted, has a tremendous impact on the hearts of its hearers; it is totally reliable and without inner contradiction. God has confirmed it through miracles, through fulfilling the predictions of its prophets, and through judgments which He brought upon its enemies. Rabus also found confirmation of this teaching in the blood of thousands of pious martyrs from Abel to

83

his own day, who had joyfully poured out their lives for the sake of this teaching.[44]

Rabus's Presuppositions: Christ against Satan

Rabus constructed his martyrology on the basis of the presupposition that Jesus Christ and His disciples always stand in conflict with Satan and his minions, a concept he shared with Flacius and every other Wittenberg student. Against the background of his eschatological conviction that the final battle for the faith was taking place in the shadow of the approaching judgment, Rabus often criticized the pope and the papal party—whom he held responsible for the Augsburg Interim—as the forces of the Antichrist. But in the prefaces of his work, his dualism set Christ or God the Father against Satan, without frequent mention of Rome. The struggle against Satan throughout the history of the church presented visible proof, Rabus believed, of the marvelous economy of Christ, by which He continued to preserve His church.[45]

Rabus began his serial meditations on the theology of martyrdom with thoughts on the significance of the title "Wondrous" conferred upon Christ in Is. 9:6. Wondrous is the incarnation of God as a human creature, and wondrous were His miracles, above all the miracle of His purchase of the church with His own blood. Also wondrous is His calling and assembling the church through the foolishness of the Gospel and the dispensing of the sacraments throughout the world. Above all, Rabus wrote, is the wondrous way, baffling to worldly wisdom, in which He preserves and rules His church in the midst of tribulation and persecution.[46] Elements of Luther's theology of the cross permeated Rabus's thinking.

Tribulation and persecution arise out of the conflict with Satan's followers, a conflict generated by the confession of the faith. Teaching and confessing God's Word, Rabus wrote, is "the highest service of God," even when the witness to its truth must be confirmed "with our blood" before an evil and wicked world. Through such witness God is glorified, His church edified and enlarged, and people are saved.[47]

Confession of the faith through martyrdom had marked the life of the church because Satan was always attacking God's Word with a number of devices. Rabus described them through the metaphor of a ship tossed about by five different storm winds: the east wind of human care and fear, of future disasters; the burdensome west wind of afflictions and sadness over the evils of the present; the anxious south wind of fickle hope and presumption regarding future fortune; the strong, raw north wind of fleshly security, based upon what it possesses at present; and finally the terrifying whirlwind of false teaching, which rages against the church.

The last of these winds increasingly concerned Rabus, for he saw an intimate connection between false teaching and persecution. He could outline the history of the church in terms of those two enemies of the church of Christ. Using a scheme formulated by Augustine, he stated that Satan assaults the church both with the deceit he used in Eden and with hostile force. Following Augustine's scheme, Rabus divided church history into three periods: that of the "violence" of the tyrannical persecutions under the Roman empire and the Arian princes of the barbarian armies; that of the "deception" of the sects (he named the Nicolaitans, Arians, Manichaeans, Donatists, and Pelagians); and the third and final period, that of the Antichrist, who combined violence with deception and who persecuted not only such late medieval figures as the Bohemian reformer of the early 15th century, John Hus, and the Florentine reformer of the late 15th century, Jerome Savonarola, but the followers of Luther as well. On the basis of his own experience and his observation of the enforcement of the Augsburg Interim, Rabus believed, the Antichrist was still pursuing them with cruelty, cunning, and violence, according to the pattern set by his murderous and lying father, the devil (John 8:44).[48]

The Threat Even amid Peace

Rabus wrote these last comments in early 1556, even though Lutherans were realizing that the Religious Peace of Augsburg, concluded in September 1555, would now insure the legal position of their faith in the lands of Lutheran princes. Although Lutheran nobles and commoners would continue to experience persecution in principalities ruled by Roman Catholic princes, legal recognition of the Augsburg Confession somewhat diminished the threat of martyrdom, which the Augsburg Interim had made so real seven years earlier. At the same time, the impact of the Counter Reformation, especially the Jesuits' advance into Germany, and the severe doctrinal disputes among German Lutherans (mentioned above) refocused Evangelical concern on other kinds of threats to the church. In succeeding prefaces to the final four German volumes of his martyrology's first edition, Rabus did not abandon the discussion of the threat to the faith posed by the sword of the tyrant as it afflicted the faithful. Papal persecution of Evangelicals was continuing in many parts of Europe; and Rabus was recording stories from France, the Netherlands, England, and other places. But his expanded perception of the dangers for the Gospel in his day led him to discuss the "deception" of Satan's minions which once again threatened proper Christian confession. Whether menaced by fire and the sword or by sweet-sounding falsehoods, the Christian faith still had to be defended by bold and forthright confession.

Confession and Discipleship under the Cross

Confession of God's true teaching was inextricably linked with the suffering and death that Christ had promised to those who confessed His holy Word and name, Rabus in 1558 told the readers of his final volume. Christ had sent His disciples out as lambs among wolves, and He promised them that they would be handed over to councils and whipped in the synagogs, led before princes and kings for His sake as His witnesses to the unbelievers (Matt. 10:16–18).[49] That could be expected because Christ Himself had suffered such. Rabus followed Luther in viewing the Christian life as one lived in Christ's footsteps, bearing the cross. He devoted the preface of his seventh volume to an explanation of Christian discipleship so described. Rabus stated, "In my opinion, whatever can be said or written about proper, pious discipleship and about its special and necessary characteristics according to the revealed Word of God is presented and demonstrated by the only-begotten Son of God Himself," especially in Christ's words, "if anyone would come after me, let him deny himself, and take up his cross, and follow me" (Matt. 16:24). Christian discipleship thus exhibits three basic characteristics: complete self-denial, "willing acceptance of the blessed cross with which the Almighty visits His own people without ceasing," and steadfastness under the cross. Against the objections the old Adam raises in opposition to this understanding of discipleship, the Christian has three particularly strong arguments, Rabus affirmed, citing the words of Christ: Whoever will preserve his life will lose it, but whoever loses his life for Christ's sake will find it. What benefit is it if a person wins the whole world and loses his own soul? When the Son of Man comes in the glory of His Father with His angels, He will reward each person according to His works (Matt. 16:25–27). Rabus provided a lengthy interpretation of this final citation in order to counter any suggestion of works-righteousness. All people, born in sin, have no abiding city in this world. They all look forward to the last day, on which they will either receive eternal joy or eternal pain according to God's just judgment. From Christian discipleship will arise that eternal joy which comes in communion with their head and redeemer. If that explanation had not eradicated the suggestion that the disciple's own works earn heaven, Rabus emphasized the unworthiness of believers on the basis of their own piety.

Complete self-denial is necessary for disciples so that they may set aside all improper presumption and false trust in their own piety and righteousness and also so that they may abandon all godless tendencies in their lives. This self-denial produces patience, and truth produces faith under the cross, which is the second characteristic of the disciples' life. But suffering the cross occasionally is not sufficient for some disciples. They must continue steadfast under all the crosses which arise in life until its end.[50]

The supreme cross, confession unto death, offends the wisdom of the Jews and the Greeks, as Rabus taught on the basis of 1 Cor. 1:18. In connection with this passage he sought to explain why Christians must suffer, even to the point of martyrdom. First, sin remains in this world, and also in the human nature of the believer. The death of the martyr reminds us that death finally must claim the sinner. Also, martyrdom, which would seem to doom the church to extinction, calls attention to the gracious care of God for His people. No human power or intelligence could have preserved the church in all its trials. Its survival demonstrates that God alone has assembled, preserved, and protected His people. The suffering of His church shows that it is God's will that His people love and obey Him not because this insures tranquillity of life, satisfaction of ambition, or other benefits of His presence, but simply because they love God and want to serve Him. The death of Christ's saints reveals that He is the only head and redeemer of His people and that the teaching which alone is God's power to save believers (Rom. 1:16) is indeed true. The disciple is not greater than his master (Matt. 10:24; John 15:20). If believers are indeed conformed to the image of God's Son so that they may receive His glory after this life, they must also be conformed to His suffering and cross here on earth (Rom. 8:17, 18).[51]

Rabus cited Paul's words in Colossians 1:24 concerning his own sufferings for Christ's sake and concluded, "For there is indeed such a sublime union between the Lord Christ, our head and shepherd, and us Christians, His members and lambs, that in body and suffering [*leib vnd leydt*], in life and death, we have and remain in an inseparable communion with each other." Luther's concept of the "joyous exchange" of Christ's righteousness for the sinner's guilt had as its corollary the earthly sharing of Christ's suffering. Rabus joined this explanation of martyrdom with elements of Luther's theology of the cross, which he had heard as he sat in Luther's lecture hall a decade earlier.[52]

Blessing in the Midst of Suffering

Rabus called his readers' attention to the positive implication of this union with Christ. All those who suffered with Christ shall certainly have joy and bliss when He reveals His glory, for He will confess before His heavenly Father all those who confess Him before other human creatures (2 Tim. 2:12; Matt. 10:32). That unspeakable joy sustains the pious through all the day of fear and agony, for they know that nothing can separate them from the love of God in Christ (Rom. 8:39).

Furthermore, based on the death of the martyrs, believers may conclude that there is life after death and that Christ will vindicate the elect in the last judgment.[53] Christians should expect to suffer for their faith since persecution of the church is nothing new or rare. From the beginning of the world, in both the Old and the New Testaments, the godless world has paid its dues to the saints in this way. "Thus, the holy cross is the proper royal color of our redeemer and highest king, Jesus Christ, not just for His own person but also for all His true servants."[54]

Finally, believers recognize that it is necessary to confront the enemies of God with a stalwart defense of the Savior's holy name through a confession given by mouth or by blood. In this way God's power and message are made perfect in weakness and foolishness, because in this way God has always triumphed over the devil's deception.[55] The deaths of the martyrs prove that Satan is still seeking to devour the church of Christ with his lies and murder, that is, with false teaching and cruel, violent tyranny (1 Peter 5:8). Knowing that Satan still is on the prowl like a raging, raving lion warns Christians to be on guard. It also provides them with comfort, since they know that Satan's instruments and tools oppose them only because they are confessing Christ. Christ will preserve His own. On behalf of the Word and truth of Christ believers must be ready to lose "body, honor, property, wife, child, home, land, life on this earth itself"— words Rabus borrowed from Luther's "A Mighty Fortress Is Our God."[56]

Martyrdom and the Theology of the Cross

Rabus commented again on the temptations of the believer to abandon the Word of God as he prepared the preface for his fifth German volume in August 1556. Lutherans held legal status in the empire now, but the temptations of seduction by false teachers remained. First, reason invents its fleshly but vain hope that Christ's kingdom will produce for His followers money, property, honor, splendor, prestige, and the like. The foolishness of the preaching of the Gospel does not create a worldly kingdom; instead, the reign of God has no specific place to which it is bound—no abiding city (Matt. 8:20, 22). Contrary to the expectations of human reason, the Gospel brings Christ's people into all sorts of tribulation and adversity. They are burdened with great worries, and ruthlessly pursued and driven here and there, as were the many saints of the Bible (Heb. 11:33–38). Here again are echoes of Luther's understanding of the Christian life under the cross. The second temptation confronting believers would seek to convince them that discipleship need not be a total devotion to Christ but only a half-hearted, fickle devotion. Against any excuse our human common sense might raise, Rabus recited a number of passages that demonstrate Christ's demand for the total allegiance of His followers (Luke 14:26; 9:62; Matt. 24:13; 2 Tim. 2:4).[57]

Rabus completed his explanation of the necessity of Christian martyrdom on the basis of 1 Peter 4 with words of consolation for those who suffer under the cross. Suffering for Christ's sake is a means by which the believer praises God. It is a mark of the presence of the Holy Spirit, who gives comfort in the midst of tribulation. There believers can give thanks even for the cross and fiery ordeal.[58]

The theme of consolation and encouragement for readers whose faith might be tested by persecution runs throughout the prefaces prepared by Rabus for the eight volumes of the first edition of his martyrology. In the first of these prefaces Rabus made it clear that he was issuing his martyrbook to give such consolation and encouragement to those who, as he wrote in 1552, believed that they still faced a serious potential for imperial and papal persecution. Only through the power of the Holy Spirit can they stand fast in the Word and resist the temptation to deny their Lord under the pressure of persecution.[59] The Word is the Holy Spirit's instrument in strengthening and preserving the believer in faith and steadfast discipleship, and Rabus used it accordingly to console and encourage his readers. A fundamental presupposition of the theology that Rabus had learned from Luther's lectures and writings permeates his theology of martyrdom: The almighty God provides for and cares for His people. The presence and power of God with those who bear the cross—the doctrine of providence—is the basis of Rabus's gospel for the martyr. Closely joined to it is his assurance that God will judge the wicked persecutors and will take His suffering people out from under the cross and bestow upon them heavenly rewards.[60]

He laid this consolation and encouragement before his readers most completely in the last preface of the first edition, (i.e., in the preface to the eighth volume), which appeared in 1558. Christ meets the weaknesses of sinful flesh in His people by providing them with a dozen sources for comfort. The Holy Trinity orders the lives of pious believers according to His gracious foreknowledge and fatherly plan for them. The proclamation of the Gospel assures them of His love. Also, God brings judgment on persecutors, as His treatment of Sodom and Gomorrah indicated. Christians are persecuted because the Holy Spirit has used them as His mouthpieces. His indwelling power and might stands by them in times of tribulation. This means suffering and shame for believers; their persecution takes place because it is of the essence of their discipleship to bear and represent the holy name and Word of Christ. Association with the Lord also comforts His people. Those who follow a suffering master expect to suffer; and they do so with confidence, comfort, and patience because of His example. This suffering clears and marks the way toward eternal bliss. Rabus also pointed out that the persecution of believers can only touch their bodies, which die and become food for worms anyway. Those who have confessed Christ before other human creatures can rest assured that He will confess that they are His before His heavenly Father. Rabus cautioned that God does not have His people risk danger for its own sake, in a frivolous way. Only when it honors Him and serves His purpose are His people driven to the ultimate witness of martyrdom.[61]

Confessing unto the End

Rabus's reason for compiling his martyrology echoed the purpose of his entire ministry: the cultivation of the Christian life, threatened as it was by the forces of Satan. The front on which those forces had to be addressed shifted while Rabus was producing his book of martyrs in the years between 1551 and 1558. Persecution by the sword receded as a possibility and concern after the conclusion of the Religious Peace of Augsburg. "Persecution" by the deceit of false teachers not only from Rome but also within the Evangelical churches and from the sects which had arisen during Rabus's lifetime had mounted. Rabus easily made the adjustment, for his goal remained the same: He wanted to foster in his readers a genuine devotion to their Lord Jesus Christ, which would boldly confess the faith. He wanted them to understand that such devotion would lead them into a life under the cross as they gave witness to what they believed. With an undiminished sense of the imminence of the eschaton, Rabus worked to prepare his readers for their own Christian service under the shadow of the approaching end of all things.

Rabus wanted to foster and nourish Christian discipleship. His theology of the cross offered a vision of the disciple's life. It was a vision increasingly remote from the lives of many Lutherans in the era of their newly-won legality, but it was a vision which some pastors and theologians found applicable to their lives. For in the era in which differing understandings of the Biblical message seemed to abound, they found continuing evidence of the necessity for confessing the faith.

Confession under Persecution

As in the case of the Interims, so also in some of those continuing controversies the confessors of the faith had to pay the price for their confessions. Particularly among the Gnesio-Lutheran party were those whose strong stand for their faith, whose propensity for confrontation rather than compromise with those whom they believed to be deceivers of God's people, had invited persecution.

Although no Gnesio-Lutherans in Germany were actually executed for their faith in the period between Luther's death and the end of the century, many suffered deprivation of office, overnight deportation from their homes and congregations, and the harassment of government officials because they refused to compromise their confession. Flacius went into exile at least four times, while his colleague at the University of Jena, Simon Musaeus, was exiled at least seven times. Their friends Cyriakus Spangenberg, Joachim Magdeburg, and others suffered more modest numbers of exiles. Because of this, Lutheranism throughout Germany provided a literature of consolation for those whose confession and rejection of compromise had cost them dearly.[62]

The most extensive of these treatments of persecution was a treatise prepared by Johann Wigand, descriptively entitled *On the Persecution of the Pious, the Exiles of the Pious, the Exiles of Hypocrites, the Martyrdoms of the Pious, Pseudomartyrs, the Flight of Ministers of the Word, Faithfulness, Apostasy, Patience.* Wigand's preface emphasized the necessity of the cross in the Christian life of confession. It promised readers that suffering would grow as the end of time approached. He perceived throughout the history of the church a certain rhythm or cycles of persecution following revivals of the proclamation of the Gospel, such as the revival the Germans had experienced under Luther's leadership. Wigand methodically examined the subjects listed in his title, using the classical Aristotelian categories as his organizational framework.

The Nature of Persecution

In accord with his usual method of investigation (which he used on a wide range of subjects), Wigand first demonstrated from Scripture that persecution indeed exists. Then he explored its definition.

92

Analyzing it on the basis of the familiar medieval division of human life into three estates, Wigand found four kinds of persecution occurring in human history: persecution that can take place in each of the ecclesiastical, political, and economic spheres, and a fourth kind of persecution that combines two or all three of these types. Persecution may take several forms: exclusion from positions in which one has formerly exercised duties, deposition from functions and offices, withdrawal of financial remuneration, subordination to one's accusers, unjust penalties from the legal system, prohibition of publication or withdrawal of the right to print one's works, deportation, prison, public mockery, torture, confiscation of property, execution, and prohibition of proper burial.

Out of his own experience Wigand was convinced that ministers of the Word of God are the most frequent victims of persecution, but pious magistrates and all outstanding people who confess the Word are subject to persecution as well. Wigand frequently used a model of logical analysis which Melanchthon had developed out of Aristotle's system of *causes* or *factors* which make up the subject under discussion. In this system the *material cause* of an action or thing is the object of whatever is being analyzed, as wood would be in an analysis of a bonfire. The *efficient cause* is the agent which makes the action happen or causes the thing to be what it is, as the person lighting it might be in the case of a bonfire. The *final* cause is the goal or purpose, warmth, for instance, in the example of the bonfire. Wigand defined the *material* cause of persecution as the affliction of ministers of God's Word and the tribulations of the laity. Persecution can be harsh or mild, secret or public. It can be imposed by heathen, Turk, or papist. Its *efficient* causes include Satan, the pope, impious magistrates, impious spouses, unjust court officials, impious jurists, apostates, and hypocrites. From his own experience Wigand could observe that magistrates are almost always involved.

People are moved to persecute Christians by any number of impulses. Prominent among them are love and zeal for a false religion, Satanic hatred, impatience over admonitions against sin, desire for revenge, love of political peace and tranquility, fear of more powerful people, and avarice. Pretexts for persecution include blasphemy and sedition—the charges the Jews of His day had made against Christ Himself—as well as false charges of apostasy, false teaching, disobedience against the discipline of the church, ambition, contempt for the fathers, and logomachy (a love of argument over words). Whatever the charges, Christians are persecuted simply because of their confession of Christ's name.

The *final* cause, the purpose or goal, of persecution is the removal of what the persecutor sees as false religion, false teaching, and false rites, as well as the establishment of peace, security, and tranquility in the land. God's purpose in permitting persecution, Wigand explained, is to provide testimony to His truth, to distinguish the pious from hypocrites in the church, to reveal Satan's hatred for the children of God, to demonstrate the presence of God with His people and the help He gives them, and to give testimony of the security of eternal life.[63]

Wigand was convinced that God sends His judgment on those who persecute His people. Spiritually He condemns them to blindness which forgets or ignores His truth, to impenitence, and to deception by false teachers, in the absence of the ministers of the Word whom they have removed from their presence. The temporal punishments visited upon persecutors, cited from Biblical and classical examples, include illness, the curse of their own children, the loss of honor, exile, and tragic death.[64]

Proper Christian Conduct under Persecution

Wigand's book contained suggestions for proper Christian conduct under persecution. Christians could endure persecution, he was certain, because they knew that their cause was good and because they stood on the testimony of the Word of God. Christians could be confident that God's favor is with them, and that He cares for them and will defeat all their enemies. In the midst of persecution Christians call upon God, have contempt for worldly things, and exhibit faithfulness, patience, and certain hope. They meditate on examples of resistance against persecution. They think about the worthiness of their calling in the sight of God and the church. They reflect on the glory awaiting them. With their suffering they glorify God, give witness to divine truth, and strengthen the weak in faith.[65]

The Question of Exile

The problems surrounding exile as an instrument of persecution were critical for Wigand precisely because he and his friends had endured this form of persecution so often. In the early 1560s, in quick succession, Wigand himself lost his position as professor at the University of Jena and then as pastor in Magdeburg because the political authorities who exercised jurisdiction over him deposed him and sent him into exile. Thus, his long section on exile is of particular interest. Much of the material is similar to that presented in the earlier section on persecution in general: Satan and his servants are responsible when Christians are sent into exile because of their legitimate profession of true Christian teaching in accordance with God's Word. Blasphemy and sedition, once again, are mentioned as pretexts for sending faithful confessors of God's Word into exile. Exile may take several forms: legal or illegal, harsher or milder. Some simply may be banished. Others suffer violent deportation; the forceable separation from wife and children; the confiscation of all their belongings; enforced exile among barbarous people, on islands, or in monasteries or prisons; condemnation to galley ships; or confinement in caves.

Wigand reviewed reasons why the minister of the Word in particular ought to resist exile. His rationale included the need to remain faithful to his call to serve specific people, the resulting denial of God's glory and truth, and the opening which exile gives for false teachers. Against those reasons he reviewed arguments that would justify acceptance of exile: Christ commanded His disciples to flee the persecutor (Matt. 10:23); one ought not tempt God by remaining where God no longer wants His minister to be; and one should not bring afflictions upon others by remaining with them as the object of persecution. Instead, the minister condemned to exile should recognize that the apostles and many ancient fathers of the church, such as Athanasius and Chrysostom, went into exile.[66]

Wigand did not develop the theology of the cross in the explicit detail that Rabus had, but Rabus's treatment of Christian suffering under persecution was far less organized and was far less developed in general than Wigand's. Nonetheless, the two shared the same perspective, based on the common orientation they had received in the early 1540s when both studied at Wittenberg. Both took it for granted that Christians confess their faith, and both therefore took persecution for granted as well. It was an inevitable part of life for those born in an age of confessing.

The Age of Confessionalism and the Augsburg Confession

The period of the Interims was truly an age of confessing. But is Hauschild correct in labeling it the opening of the "age of confessionalism"? He is, and for several reasons. Out of the struggles of this period came the confessional groups that were forming in Germany, parallelling developments throughout western Christendom. These confessional groups were forming around new definitions of their own message and mission, as the battlefields and martyrdoms made more urgent the task of defining why these churches should exist at all.

Among the most important elements in the forming of these confessional groups was their choice of a secondary authority for the life of the church. The Scriptures have at least theoretically claimed primary place in the system of authority of most Christian churches throughout history. This was certainly true among the Lutherans. However, the new confessional church bodies of the 16th century were compelled to decide what their chief guide for interpreting the Scriptures and applying them to the life of the church would be. Apart from the Roman Catholics, the secondary authority of the medieval Western church—popes and councils and bishops—would no longer serve. Lutherans eventually turned to documents—the ancient creeds, confessions, and catechisms composed as they experienced the unfolding of the Reformation. This process began with the confession of faith at Augsburg and culminated in the Formula of Concord. In this latter document the Lutherans distinguished between Scripture and those writings of ancient and modern teachers that could never be put on a par with Holy Scripture but nonetheless could serve as expositions of the Christian faith and would, in turn, serve as standards for the public teaching of God's Word (FC, Ep 2, 6).

In defending the authority of the Augsburg Confession, Nikolaus Selnecker, one of the Formula's authors, carefully distinguished the ultimate norm and rule for guiding the formulation of dogma (the Scriptures) from secondary vehicles of doctrinal authority in the church. The Scriptures judge all teachers and teachings. But, he added, in the wake of Luther's restoration of the light of the Gospel, the Augsburg Confession assumed a key role in governing teaching;

and it was joined in that role by the Apology of the Augsburg Confession, the Smalcald Articles, Luther's Catechisms, and finally the Formula of Concord.

Selnecker argued that these were not the Word of God but faithfully represented Scripture, which is that Word and thus is the only authority, canon, norm, and rule for teaching and faith. Because these contemporary documents, along with the three ancient creeds, represent what Scripture teaches—and what the Holy Spirit had taught through Martin Luther—they serve the church as a secondary authority for public teaching.[67]

Luther as a Secondary Authority

The church has always found secondary sources for authority, sources which gave direction to and set parameters for the theologians who exercise tertiary or everyday authority for the pastors, teachers, and laity of the church. In the Middle Ages councils and popes had served as the secondary sources, the prime interpreters of Scripture. With the outbreak of the Reformation, at least for those in the Wittenberg movement, Luther served as the most important of the secondary sources of authority for his followers (along with the analogy of the faith—a consensus on what of the ancient church's teaching had indeed been faithful to Scripture). Luther's doctrine of the living voice of the Gospel—specifically, that God has placed His power in human language—permitted his followers to see in his preaching and writing an interpretation of the Biblical Word which would govern the theologians, pastors, and teachers as they carried out their callings from God to spread His Word.

When Luther died, the authority to interpret Scripture—which he had often exercised for and among his followers—did not immediately die. There were determined efforts to use the corpus of his writings to establish Biblical truth. But some of his followers also sought a worthy living successor for Luther as a secondary authority in the church. His mantle seemed to fall on Melanchthon's shoulders, even though others, such as Amsdorf, were also nominated for this honor and task.[68] However, in the eyes of many in the Wittenberg movement, Melanchthon proved himself unworthy and incapable of the exercise of such authority. As Hans Christoph von Hase comments, regarding Melanchthon's failure to attack the Augsburg Interim more publicly and more sharply, "Flacius recognized very clearly: if an ecclesiastical leader denies the public exercise of his office, then he thereby loses his authority completely."[69]

Where could this secondary authority—which the church always needs in its ongoing formulation of the Word of God for its current situation—find a place in the Lutheran churches? Popes had failed; Luther had died and left no successor as an authoritative voice. It was only natural for those heirs of the Biblical humanism of Wittenberg to turn to documents. God had placed His prophetic and apostolic Word authoritatively in the Scriptures. The oral confession of Augsburg had taken form in a document. Luther's message could be found in succinct form in his Smalcald Articles and his Catechisms. Where better to find the prime interpretation of the Biblical message than in the public confessional documents of the Wittenberg movement? The Lutheran churches replaced popes and councils with *The Book of Concord* when Luther was no longer present to guide them.

In the years following his death, no other voice of authority raised against the threat of the Interims had sufficient stature to command the place of Luther for itself. The confessional documents therefore assumed preeminence. Because they themselves were regulated by Holy Scripture, they were able to serve as the rule for public teaching. They could serve as a secondary basis for continued confessing of the faith, which remained a necessary part of the church's life.

4

Confessing in Controversy: The Habit of Confession in the Late Reformation

The Interims passed into history. With the Truce of Passau in 1552 they were retired, and with the Religious Peace of Augsburg in 1555 they died. Yet the need to confess the faith did not die with them. Roman Catholic determination to eradicate "the Lutheran pest" remained stronger than ever. The challenges to Lutheran teaching from Calvinists and Schwenckfelders, Anabaptists and Antitrinitarians, elicited confession from Luther's heirs. The internal disputes that wracked the Wittenberg movement itself imposed the necessity of clear confession upon the Lutherans. Confessing the faith had to continue. It did so primarily in a defensive mode, as fears of a decisive assault on the faith outweighed hopes for successfully spreading the Lutheran confession. In such situations Lutherans disagreed with each other as to how the faith could best be confessed and as to what specifically constituted a clear and proper confession of the faith. Therefore, in personal statements, in controversy, and in newly-composed confessions Lutheran theologians struggled again to define what was meant by confessing the faith.

Conflicting Strategies for Confessing the Faith

In the period of the Interims the Gnesio-Lutherans especially had practiced a forthright confession of the faith; so it was among them that discussion of a strategy for confession took place in the years after the Interims had been set aside. The Gnesio-Lutheran discussions grew out of concrete situations. One case arose in the city of Erfurt at the end of the 1560s. In this case Gnesio-Lutherans disagreed with each other. Both Lutherans and Roman Catholics had retained churches in Erfurt, and members of both confessions served on the faculty of the city's university. The Roman Catholics had continued to administer the university even though more than 40 years earlier the population of the city had become largely Evangelical. In 1569 the university faculty elected its first Evangelical rector, Johann Gallus, who was also a pastor in Erfurt.

The office of rector was traditionally bestowed with great ceremony, including a breakfast with the faculty at the new rector's home, a procession through the streets of the city by the Roman clergy, and a celebration of the mass in the cathedral. Gallus believed that these ceremonies were mere formalities that would not suggest any compromise of faith on his part. He accepted the election and reported it to the Senior of the Evangelical ministerium, Andreas Poach (1516–85), who also served as a professor of Evangelical theology within the university's liberal arts faculty. Poach, a staunch supporter of Flacius and his Magdeburg colleagues during the height of the Interims controversies, objected. The ministerium divided on the issue.

Poach based his argument on such Bible passages as Ps. 94:20; 2 Cor. 6:14–18; 2 Thess. 3:6; Titus 3:10; 2 John 10 and 11; and Rev. 18:4. He argued that participation in such university ceremonies with Roman clergy would betray the Evangelical faith. Ten years earlier, someone at the electoral Saxon court had complained to Poach about the city's toleration of Romanism. At about the same time the ministerium had received an invitation to participate in the installation of a Roman Catholic rector for the university. That invitation had been declined because, the ministerium argued, such participation would compromise the clear confession of the faith. Based on that precedent, Poach now instructed Gallus either to insist on new forms for the installation that would not suggest that Romanists and Lutherans could stand side by side as if in agreement or to decline the election. Gallus refused to comply with Poach. Gallus's brother-in-law, Georg Silberschlag, also supported Poach.

Opposing Poach and supporting Gallus was the prominent Gnesio-Lutheran associate of the Magdeburgers, Johannes Aurifaber (1516–75), who led others who backed Gallus.[1] Aurifaber and Gallus received support for their position also from Gnesio-Lutheran friends at the University of Jena: Johannes Wigand, Tilemann Hesshus, and Johann Friedrich Coelestin. The city council, too, supported Gallus's position. It decided that participation in external or secular formalities connected with essentially nonreligious matters—such as the installation of a rector of the municipal university—was not a matter of confession. Gallus was installed as rector.

The dispute continued to simmer, and in 1571 two arbitrators from the ministerium at Halle were called to Erfurt: the city's ecclesiastical superintendent, Sebastian Boetius, and his colleague, Caspar Cantangiesser. Their decision found that both sides were equally dedicated to confessing the "pure teaching of the holy Gospel and condemning and criticizing the errors and abuses of the papacy." They found that Gallus and his supporters had made no concessions and had not committed any abuses in their table fellowship with the papal party. The Halle delegation agreed with Gallus that a distinction between associations in "outward, profane matters" and the confession of the Gospel is necessary. They found that the activities surrounding the university's installation of a new rector fell into the former category.[2]

During 1571 Poach and his ally Silberschlag kept the matter alive, the latter through published sermons. In an introduction to a sermon of the church father Cyril, Silberschlag warned against compromising with the world and leading oneself to ruin for the sake of earthly and fleshly things. In his last sermon before his death, he treated Gen. 35:2–7 and condemned those who would retain false and foreign gods in their own houses. He applied this principle to the city of Erfurt, which, Silberschlag accused, was retaining remnants of papal idolatry within its walls. He warned of God's wrath to come.[3] Silberschlag died at an early age in February 1572, and Poach took the occasion to attack very sharply both the Roman Catholics and his "compromising" brethren in the ministerium.[4] In the midst of this bitter dispute, which even saw Poach's followers announcing from their pulpits the excommunication of fellow pastors, Poach resigned his pastorate (as a result of indirect pressure from the city council) and left the city.[5]

Defining the Confessional Situation

Not long before Poach left the city, Hesshus republished a section of a work from the previous year, undoubtedly because it contributed to the case for Gallus's participation in the university festivities. The original work was entitled *On the Confession of the Name of Jesus Christ before Humankind*. It dealt with a range of problems relating to the confession of the faith, largely occasioned by the efforts of Jakob Andreae to unite Lutherans through a program of concession, compromise, and concealment of differences. It could well be that Hesshus included the issue posed in the tract precisely because of the current situation in Erfurt. He defined that issue with the title of the newly reprinted tract, *Question: Whether a Faithful Christian May Have Civil Communion (and Eat and Drink, etc.) With Non-Christians, Such as Jews, Turks, Heathen, or with Publicly Identified Heretics, Blasphemers, and Idol Worshipers, or Such as Enemies of the Sacraments, Papists, Anabaptists, Monks and Papal Priests, or with Public Epicureans and Sinners, Who are Stuck in Conscious Adultery and Other Blasphemies, The Answer of Doctor Tilemann Hesshus*.

Hesshus presumed with Paul that Christians dare not be called the brothers of those who practice immorality or are greedy (1 Cor. 5:11) and that they will not welcome or greet those who do not abide in Christ's teaching (2 John 9–11). Such situations called for clear confession of the faith. On the other hand, Hesshus noted Christ's continual associations with the Pharisees, who were steeped in error, and with public sinners and tax collectors. Paul had no objection to believers accepting invitations to dinner from unbelievers (1 Cor. 10:27).

Therefore, Hesshus laid out a number of guidelines for answering the question posed by his title. First, when the situation demands clear confession of the faith, Christians must separate themselves from unbelievers. The servants of the pope—bishops, canons, monks, and priests—like to invite Evangelical citizens to eat with them and to have them as friends so that these Roman leaders can blunt the condemnation of their false teaching by the Evangelicals. In such instances Joseph refused to eat with the Egyptians (Gen. 43:32; but the situation actually seems to have been the reverse, for the Egyptians' custom forbade eating with others), and the Jews refused commerce with the Samaritans (John 4:9) and with unclean substances of all kinds (Acts 10:14). "Therefore, when it looks as if confession will be obscured through an action, such as eating with idol worshipers, we should abstain from such an action and flee such hospitality."[6]

Hesshus's second guideline instructed Christians not to associate with those who had been excommunicated and failed to repent. Third, when offense might be given to the weak by such associations, they are to be avoided (Matt. 18:6; 1 Cor. 8:1–13). Fourth, it is also obvious that whenever such an invitation to association, particularly at table, would lead to gluttony, drunkenness and debauchery, it must be avoided. Otherwise believers are free to eat and to associate with non-Christians and heretics. Such association may even turn out to be a work of love, for it may be possible to call them to repentance in the course of such associations, as many Biblical examples demonstrate. Hesshus warned of the temptation to deny Christ in such situations and of the condemnation that comes upon all hypocrisy. He also reminded his readers that, in eating and drinking and in whatever believers do, all should be done for the glory of God (1 Cor. 10:31).[7]

Both Poach and his opponents believed that Hesshus had supported their side in the Erfurt controversy. Although Hesshus supported Gallus's right to participate in the university's inaugural ceremonies, as he did, Hesshus also shared Poach's view of the need to confess forthrightly when the truth and clarity of the Word of God were under threat of being clouded and obscured. Both realized the importance of confessing the faith not only through clear words but also through unambiguous acts. Both knew the importance of symbolic action. Nevertheless, Hesshus did present a more nuanced, sophisticated analysis of the cases in which confession is demanded. He did so by carefully distinguishing between confession through separation, on the one hand, and, on the other hand, confession through association, which shows Christian love and strives to induce repentance. He distinguished situations in which association obscures the truth of God's Word and situations in which such association furthers the confession of His Word. Hesshus believed in confession for the sake of the faith and its propagation, not for the sake of self-defense or self-justification. He believed that judgments must be made regarding the impact of one's words and actions as well as their intention, so that confession accomplishes its goal of calling the erring to repentance and to the Gospel. He was working out the principles that his colleagues at Magdeburg had enunciated during the Interims controversies in the era begun by the Peace of Augsburg of 1555.

Toward a Definition of Confession

Others who had studied at Wittenberg in the 1540s found occasion to publish similar explanations of and admonitions concerning the need in this period for ongoing confession of the faith. The most thoroughgoing and carefully organized of these analyses was that of Hesshus' close friend, Johannes Wigand.

"Just as the golden sun, ascending above the horizon, quickly spreads the rays of its light and delivers a clear day to the hemisphere, so wherever true faith ascends in the hearer through the Holy Spirit, there good works, both inward and outward, follow and reveal themselves."[8] So Wigand began his treatise *On the Confession of Divine Teaching and Necessary Actions*. He composed it in 1569, at a critical juncture in the course of the disputes between Wigand's Gnesio-Lutheran colleagues and their Philippist opponents.

For the better part of a year Wigand himself had been participating in the Altenburg Colloquy, designed to reconcile the Philippists and Gnesio-Lutherans. This effort collapsed, in part over the issue of the clarity of confessing the faith by means of condemning the errors that threatened it. Wigand and his colleagues from the University of Jena insisted on detailed treatment of the positive expression of Biblical teaching on controverted points. In addition, they believed firmly that the truth on those points could not become clear if the errors giving rise to controversy were not carefully set forth and refuted.[9]

At the same time, in 1568–1569, Jakob Andreae had come to north Germany with a program for ending the disputes that had torn the Lutheran churches apart. He was representing his own prince, Duke Christoph of Württemberg, and the efforts of princes and other Evangelical political leaders to reestablish a united front among the Lutheran estates. Andreae's program at this time emphasized uniting at the lowest common denominator (from Wigand's point of view), and so Wigand was fiercely opposed to Andreae's principle of "forgetting" the divisive issues, a program summarized with the word "amnesty."[10] Against such attempts at compromise, Wigand asserted the necessity of confession of the faith.

In doing so, he simply expanded upon the principles he previously had cited in criticizing attempts at compromise at the time of the Interims. In 1552 he had written that, as valuable as people who take the middle ground and attempt to work out compromises may be in political affairs, they have no place whatsoever in matters relating to the faith. "For God demands confession of sound teaching and of correct worship practices from all, without distinction of gender, estate, or status."[11]

Hesshus indicated that he was writing his *On the Confession of the Name of Jesus Christ* for the same reasons: to oppose those who wanted to compromise the confession of the faith, which he pointedly defined as "the name of Jesus Christ," the core of the faith he held. He criticized "the libertine sect, which agrees with the Adiaphorists and holds that there is a special freedom of the Spirit that permits hanging the mantle to the wind and adapting to the times, so that no one is angered by the confession of the truth and no one brings himself or his loved ones into danger, but rather says and does everything that the godless tyrants want, no matter whether it is forbidden in God's Word." He also condemned "the gang which calls itself the Household of Love, which acts in even cruder fashion and not only permits hypocrisy and outrageous fellowship with papists and other idolators and tyrants, but even allows every kind of sin and vice, if only the conscience does not regard it as sin"— a popular description of the Dutch Family of Love, a sect which kept its identity hidden from governmental authorities and was accused of a libertine way of life.[12] Hesshus noted that this error was to be found also among the Zwinglians, such as his former opponent in the dispute over the Lord's Supper in Bremen, Albert Hardenburg, who "acknowledged publicly that he had kept his view hidden for seven years." But in 1571, when he wrote his treatise, Hesshus was battling the undermining of stalwart confession by Jakob Andreae. Hesshus believed that Andreae was trying to invent a new way to minimize error and to convince people that differing interpretations of the faith could stand together. This, Hesshus charged, denied the name of Christ.[13]

Against this background, Wigand and Hesshus each attempted a synthesis of the Gnesio-Lutheran understanding of proper confes-

ɔf the faith. Wigand began by defining the term in Biblical
᠁. Confession has three meanings: to offer testimony of the truth;
to praise God with a recognition of and testimony to the truth; and
to acknowledge one's sins, be sorrowful over them, and to pray for
grace.

Wigand focused on the first definition in this treatise. He identified the *activity* of confessing the faith with *teaching* what has been
revealed and handed down by God—"than which nothing is more
important, nothing more precious, nothing more salutary." This
testimony of the truth involves both what is taught in the church
and how its worship is conducted, he insisted—against the background of attempts in the Augsburg Interim to undermine Evangelical confession through changes in worship practices. Wigand
acknowledged that such practices are not matters of confession in
and of themselves. But when confession is called for in the face of
threats to the faith involving these practices, then they too become
vehicles by which the faith must be defended and confessed.[14] Hesshus added for his readers that public witness is given through works
of love as well.

The Cause of Confession

Wigand emphasized that the ability to confess comes not from flesh
and blood but from God (Matt. 16:17; Matt. 10:20; Phil. 1:29; Rom.
10:14–17; Ps. 51:17; 2 Cor. 3:5). His command is the fundamental
"effective cause" of confessing the faith. The immediate cause of
confession is "glowing faith in the reborn heart, sending forth rays
of its light with an unrestrained tongue. For faith is the fountain and
wellspring of confession."[15] Hesshus reiterated this point in his commentary on Romans 10:10: "Faith produces a lively and clear confession of God's name, for it is the nature of faith, when it apprehends
true righteousness in the Word, that it bursts forth in oral confession,
praising and celebrating the name of Christ, giving witness to its
delight in God, desiring to lead all people to Christ and to propagate
His kingdom."

Against those who would suggest that the good work of confessing the faith might be meritorious, Hesshus firmly stated that
confession is not a "cause, instrument or part of salvation, but an
effect and a fruit" of God's saving action.[16]

Wigand's colleague during his student days at Wittenberg, Cyriakus Spangenberg, had echoed these views in his own preaching on Rom. 10:10 and 1 Thess. 1:6–10. He explained to his congregation that the joyful reception of God's Word produces a confession of its content, a confession which spreads God's message and demonstrates its impact in daily life. This confession sounds forth like a trumpet and makes God's Word manifest like the scent of a fragrant flower. There is no surer witness of faith in Christ than oral public confession, he stated in his Romans commentary, for such confession acknowledges that Christ is Lord. There can be no faith without confession, and no confession without faith.[17] Spangenberg's protégé, Johannes Scheitlich, reminded his readers that this faith arises out of God's pledge in Holy Baptism, which was for Scheitlich one of several bases for the believer's daily confession of faith.[18]

Faith is moved to confess, Wigand believed, by God's command, by God's glory and His love for His human creatures, by the need to edify the church, by a good conscience, by Christ's promise of eternal glory for those who confess His name before others (Matt. 10:32), and by fear of God's punishment for those who disobey God's command to confess.[19] Wigand often combined the motivations of Law and Gospel, as he did in this case, and thereby blurred the distinction between the two. So did Spangenberg as he discussed *Some Lofty and Important Reasons Why Every Christian, of Whatever Estate He May Be, is Duty-Bound at Every Time, But Especially Now, To Make Public Confession of His Faith and Teaching, Orally, and If Possible, Also in Writing.* Spangenberg noted that God moves believers to both oral and written confession of the faith through His command that His name be honored and through His comforting promise to be with His people. Spangenberg preferred the latter motivation, but he added that if the promise would not move the Christian, then the threat should.[20]

Spangenberg and Wigand believed that God's promise—and His threat—place the confession of the faith in daily life within the larger perspective of His entire plan for the propagation of His Word. In Wigand's personal confession of the faith, published in 1582, the eschatological nature of confession in the presence of God is made clear. In the preface to this personal confession Wigand wrote that his little book was a public testimony before my dear God in heaven and before all Christians on earth, that by God's gift, blessing, and aid I have presented and confessed the only one, correct, true, salutary, and beneficial teaching, as I have heard and learned it from God's Word and from the sainted Luther's mouth and writings, that I want to stand upon this teaching and remain and persist in it until by God's grace I lie in the grave and my bed of rest (to that end may God, who has created and redeemed me, give me aid), Amen.[21]

Wigand's entire ministry took place under threat and against a background of eschatological expectation. It is little wonder that he thought of confession in such terms.

Who Must Confess

All Christians are commanded to confess, Wigand urged, as he set forth the "material cause" through which God makes confession of the faith known. Even the lowly should confess, for God uses the weak of this world to accomplish His will (Ps. 8:1–2, Matt. 11:25). Against the background of the threat from the Interims to his understanding of the Christian faith, Wigand insisted upon the necessity of confession by laity and clergy alike. Pastors are called to preach and teach in a specific location, but all Christians are called to confess the faith wherever it stands under the threat of corruption and falsification.[22]

Hesshus agreed, although he knew that because of the inborn weakness of the sinful human nature people were likely to shy away from the risks that confessing involves for them and their families. He warned that a pagan, Epicurean sense of security lures simple, weak Christians away from faithful confession. He rejected the suggestion of the fourth-century church father, Epiphanius, that public confession of the truth is not always necessary, especially in times of persecution, as long as the believer has faith in the heart. For Hesshus, that alluring view is untenable. All have been encouraged to confess by Christ's promise to confess before His Father those who confess His name (Matt. 10:32), regardless of whether they may offend government authorities or parents thereby (Matt. 10:37). No one can remain silent in good conscience when there is opportunity to tell of the great and boundless benefits that God has given His people in Jesus Christ.

To demonstrate this, Hesshus rehearsed a number of examples from the Bible and from the early church. He reminded his readers of the terrible fate encountered by contemporaries who had failed to remain faithful to their confession of the faith. Johannes Hoffmeister suffered the fate of living with a bad conscience. He confessed before his death that he had denied the Gospel despite his conscience. A "Dr. Kraus from Halle" and the Italian Protestant apostate, Francesco de Spiera, both committed suicide in despair because they had denied the faith. Likewise the former Lutheran pastor of Mansfeld county, Stephan Agricola, who became a Roman Catholic, threw himself overboard in the Adriatic Sea while on a mission to Rome—"out of despair," Hesshus reported, "a terrible judgment of God." To prevent such a fate, all Christians should confess their faith, "not only the preachers and the learned, but also their hearers, who know the joy of the Gospel."[23]

Spangenberg had written his entire treatise on confession around that point: Every congregation and every Christian not only have the privilege but also the command of God "to judge all teaching according to God's Word, to confess the truth, and to refute error." Nowhere, according to Spangenberg, did God command waiting for a synod, or a council, or the approval of government officials in confessing and defending the faith.[24]

Andreas Schoppe, Spangenberg's colleague in Mansfeld county, offered readers 23 reasons why the laity should confess the faith publicly. He cited Christ (Matt. 23:10) in defending the laity's ability to speak publicly without submitting to clerical authority. He also cited Luther; Melanchthon; their colleague and Wittenberg town pastor, Johannes Bugenhagen; Jakob Andreae; and another Wittenberg graduate, the north German pastor Christoph Fischer; as well as the examples of Moses, Joshua, David, and other Old Testament prophets and teachers who admonished the people of God to examine what they were being taught and to reject false teachers. He criticized opponents for making the laity into "mere geese and people without the Spirit." The devil is trying to exclude the laity from spiritual matters and thus take away their faith, he argued; that is clearly an arrow of the Antichrist. Since all Christians are priests and kings before God (1 Peter 2:9), and since lay people read the same

Word in Scripture as do pastors, they should indeed be able to confess and judge the teaching of the church publicly. They must be prepared to give an answer to all (1 Peter 3:15), for they cannot bring others to the true religion if they are not confessing and judging the church's teaching themselves. Schoppe rejected the argument that this would be interference in the office of the public ministry.[25]

Another protégé of Spangenberg, Sebastian Krell, distinguished five levels at which Christians confess the faith. The first is that of those who are weak in the faith and hardly know the catechism. Other believers must pray for such people that they are able to make a confession of their faith. Second, there are those simple people who know the catechism and can use it to testify to the faith and to refute error. Third, there are those pastors and deacons, and many outside the office of the public ministry, who know the chief articles of the faith well. Above them are the superintendents of the church and the theological professors. Finally, the last level is that of temporal authorities.[26]

The role of temporal authorities in the public confession of the church was a particularly controversial point during the Interims and the disputes that followed, because the princes and city councils of Lutheran lands had indeed claimed for themselves a major role in the life of the churches in their principalities or towns. But they had not always supported their theologians in ways which these theologians believed served God faithfully.

Therefore, the Gnesio-Lutherans issued a two-sided warning to the Evangelical public. First, the people of God must confess the faith—even in opposition to their rulers when they oppose God. Echoing the Gnesio-Lutheran resistance theory formulated at Magdeburg in 1550, Spangenberg made this point in the preface of Scheitlich's tract. There he condemned courtiers and "some horrible clever lawyers," as well as certain theologians, who were trying to frustrate proper confession of the faith.[27]

Second, Gnesio-Lutherans stated, Christian rulers are obliged to confess their faith publicly. Wigand specifically singled out magistrates—"nursemaids for the church of God" (Is. 49:23)—as those who must confess.[28] In his pamphlet *On the Confession of the Name of Jesus Christ*, in its dedication to Wolff von Koteritz, chancellor at the ducal Saxon court in Weimar, Hesshus noted that the mighty

110

are tempted to blow with the wind on matters of faith. He insisted that all are obliged to confess, including political counselors and princes, as did the Old Testament kings.[29]

When to Confess

Spangenberg also insisted that Christians must confess the faith at all times. In response to those who suggested that no public confession was necessary at times when opponents were not pressing for a confession, he answered that God always presses for confession in order that His Word may come to unbelievers and so that false teaching can be revealed. Against those who argued that sufficient confession of the faith had already been given, he answered that the praise of God, as it takes place in confession of the faith, should continually be offered and renewed. He lauded the Augsburg Confession and its Apology, as well as the ancient creeds; but he pointed out that like the Scriptures, these would be silenced and perverted if believers did not confess afresh.[30] Like Hesshus and Wigand, Spangenberg believed that confessing the faith should be the believer's way of life.

The Source of Confession

Wigand continued his treatise with a discussion of the characteristics of public confession and its "formal causes." First, the believer's confession of the faith must always be congruent with God's Word, "the norm of true confession, as it is comprehended in the writings of the prophets and apostles." Wigand expanded on what it is that guides one to know how to make the proper confession of the faith:

> We testify publicly and forthrightly before God and the whole world that we embrace and avow with our whole heart the Word of God handed down and comprehended in the books written by the hands of the prophets and apostles, and in the three creeds, Apostolic, Nicene, and Athanasian, in the Augsburg Confession which was presented to Charles V and the whole Roman empire in 1530, its Apology, the Smalcald Articles, and the writings of Luther, as well as the Confutation of the most illustrious dukes of Saxony. We reject whatever disagrees with this norm, and whatever agrees with it we accept and approve.[31]

111

Here Wigand did not distinguish between the primary authority of Scripture and the secondary authority of the creeds and 16th-century confessions. The Word of God was to be confessed out of and under the guidance of all of them.

Wigand's second characteristic of proper confession is certainty. No wavering voice can properly confess the faith. Hesshus flatly stated that a confession issued with doubting tone, fork-tongued and artful, is worse than a public denial. Public denial is open and straightforward; an unstable confession deceives the simple.[32] Furthermore, Wigand affirmed, confession of the faith is a necessary part of the Christian life, and it always involves rejection of errors and those who teach errors (the point under dispute with the Philippists over "amnesty," or forgetting who it was who had taught falsely). Hesshus was even sharper in his insistence on the necessity of specific condemnation of whatever opposes the truth that believers confess.[33]

Wigand further insisted that confession must be clear, forthright, and frank. Confessors should be gentle and modest, not coercive, harsh, or abusive in their testimony to the Word. Confessors must also be constant, persevering even in the face of danger and threat. Faith always governs the confession; and prayer for God's aid, presence, and direction always accompany that confession. Such aid comes through the Holy Spirit's action in Word and Sacrament, Wigand assured his readers. He concluded his list of the characteristics of confession by emphasizing again that confession involves both the teaching and the worship practices of the church, that it can be done in various ways (orally, in writing, through deeds), and that suffering is the companion of confession.[34]

The Purpose of Confession

Wigand identified the "final cause" or purpose of confession in a list of seven goals that parallels his summary of the reasons for it. Confessing the faith will proclaim, preserve, and propagate divine truth. It will give glory to God and edify His church. It will fend off the enemies and persecutors of the faith. It will demonstrate that the believer has a good conscience before God. It will win temporal and eternal rewards. It will stave off temporal and eternal punishments.[35]

Spangenberg had his own list of reasons for confessing the faith, which also expressed his goals in confession. First, through His command to honor His name and through His comforting promise, God moves His people to confess; He wants them to be confessing His name and His Gospel at all times so that unbelievers may hear this confession and so that false teaching may be uncovered. Second, confession is necessary because Christians cannot keep quiet about the truth. They want to give witness to their faith, and confession is the first fruit of faith (Rom. 10:9; Ps. 116:10; 2 Cor. 4:13). Third, Christians confess because of their own need and the need of others: confession strengthens and clarifies faith and wards off false teaching in the life of the confessor and in the lives of others as well. Spangenberg further urged Christians to confess because the act of confession honors God and His Word: It spreads the truth; it uncovers error and falsification of the truth; it sharpens the content of the confession; it proves one's love for friend and foe alike; it restores the offended, timid, and weak in faith; it strengthens the faithful and makes them joyful; it leads the doubting to certain ground; it converts the erring and the deceived; it brings shame upon the stubborn and those who wantonly adhere to false teaching; and it confirms the bond of love among the faithful.[36] Spangenberg's pastoral concern centered around the Word's effect on Christ's people and the necessity of preventing the deception of the devil and his cohorts from leading believers astray.[37]

Case Studies in Confessing the faith

Hesshus applied his principles in a series of case studies posed for his readers of *On the Confession of the Name of Jesus.* The first raised the question "whether a Christian who lives among the papists may have his child baptized by the papistic priest or pastor." He rejected that possibility since "the use of the sacraments is a sign and public confession regarding the church to which we belong." No fellowship of such a sort was permitted with an "idolatrous" church (1 Cor. 10:21). Because the Word of God was present, there could be no doubt that the Roman Catholic baptism was valid. But God has forbidden a common confession with those who pervert the Gospel. Here Hesshus distinguished the power of the Word of God, dependent on nothing in the one who speaks it, from its use as a sign of agreement in the content of the confession. Hesshus believed that his position was supported by the example of the ancient church when believers refused Arian baptism and ordination, and by Luther's admonition to the Christians of Frankfurt in which he opposed sacramental fellowship with the Zwinglians.[38]

Hesshus further asked, "If a Christian wants to have his deceased family members buried under the papacy, how should he proceed? May he without injury to his conscience invite the mass-priests to perform the burial and pay them some money so that they do not say masses for the soul or do other idolatrous acts?" Hesshus regarded such a possibility as hypocrisy. Some had argued that, since it is not a sin to give a highway man money if one is held up in the forest, so in necessity a person could have Roman Catholic priests perform a funeral service and pay them for it. Hesshus reminded his readers that burial by Roman Catholic priests is a confessional act because it involves a service of the Word. Similarly, Hesshus rejected the possibility that a Christian bridegroom could permit his marriage to be conducted by a Roman Catholic pastor. Even though marriage is a temporal matter, and thus a Christian can accept an invitation to a Roman Catholic wedding, the confirmation of marriage by the minister of the Word is a spiritual matter. That should be done, Hesshus insisted, by one who believes the Gospel and teaches God's Word soundly and purely. Hesshus cited the example of a prince of his acquaintance (probably one of the dukes of Saxony, John Frederick the Middler or John William) who refused to be married by a "Zwinglian preacher" and thus denounced the Zwinglians as "godless false teachers."[39]

Hesshus likewise rejected the possibility of receiving the Lord's Supper from Roman Catholic priests because without the cup the Sacrament is not present. If a Roman priest were to offer the Lord's Supper according to Christ's command, in both kinds, the believer still should not receive it, for such a priest is mocking God and the world by refusing to confess his faith openly and by refusing to adhere to the Augsburg Confession.[40]

Some guilds had retained medieval practices regarding observations for the dead, often because an endowment remained for the purpose of sponsoring such observations. Hesshus advised Evangelical Christians to leave the guilds rather than continue practicing these pagan customs, thus burdening their conscience with a false confession of the Gospel. He also rejected any sacramental fellowship with Zwinglians, Calvinists, and the like; and he reviewed briefly why the compromise in adiaphora required by the Interims was a denial of the faith. He added references to the works of Flacius, Westphal, Gallus, Wigand, and others.[41] Then he turned to the question of table fellowship with unbelievers and heretics of various kinds, which touched upon the Erfurt situation.[42] Here he defined a kind of association with people who did not share the true confession of the faith, which did not deny his own act of confession. Hesshus evaluated the impact of each case and determined whether the particular practice under question suggested a denial of the Gospel. For Hesshus, the way one's faith is to be confessed depends at least in part on the effect of the confessional words or actions.

Hesshus, like his own associates and his long-time acquaintances Wigand and Spangenberg, believed that the Christian faith naturally flows into a confession of the faith. As at Augsburg, so in the daily life of the Lutheran Christian, confession of the faith was a gift from God, an opportunity to serve Him and to love the neighbor, an expression of the trust binding the believer to Christ.

Necessity Produces New Confessions

A perspective such as held by Wigand, Spangenberg, and Hesshus led them to expect and even risk persecution because they believed that confessing the faith was a central part of their way of life as Lutherans. They continued to believe that the end of all things was approaching, and this eschatological sense of urgency drew them to protect as well as to proclaim their faith. Therefore, Lutherans continued to confess not only in deeds but also in writing, specifically the writing of new confessions.

Confessions in Different Forms

The term *confession* became a popular title for personal statements regarding issues under dispute, on the model of Luther's "Great" *Confession on the Lord's Supper* of 1528. Such individual confessions served a variety of purposes among Lutheran theologians during the later years of the 16th century. Some issued their confessions simply as a last will and testament of piety, as seems to have been the case with the blind pastor of Erfurt, Caspar Angelander, whose confession took form in his collection of comments on more than 30 doctrinal topics, cited from Luther, Melanchthon, and other reformers.[43] Other personal confessions are in fact personal statements by individuals or small groups caught up in the midst of controversy, some serving as quasi-legal declarations of belief in the face of ecclesiastical authorities, others representing part of the ongoing polemic over a certain issue. Some of these later turned the title *confession* into a synonym for a doctrinal treatise.[44]

The doctrinal conflicts between the Gnesio-Lutherans and their opponents, both Philippists and Reformed, produced position statements by a ministerium or by a theological faculty regarding points at issue. The faculty of the University of Jena issued confessions to defend its position in controversy with Philippist opponents in the wake of their unsuccessful colloquy at Altenburg in 1568–69.[45] The controversy over the Lord's Supper especially brought forth such confessions.[46]

The model of Augsburg also continued to shape Lutheran ecclesiastical life in the later 16th century, resulting in formal, authoritative confessions. These were published in a variety of situations by groups of Lutherans and groups of Lutheran theologians during the third quarter of the 16th century. These confessions publicly declared the teaching of Lutheran churches under challenge from society and government authority, in the spirit of Augsburg. But they also began transforming the Lutheran concept of confession.[47]

The Gnesio-Lutherans also found several occasions that required new confessional documents. Confessing the faith in confrontation with error marked their style of churchmanship. The challenge of opposing both false teaching and hostile political forces brought forth a number of confessions from several groups within this party. Too much can be made of the distinction between *kerygma* and *didache*. Nonetheless, the kerygmatic style, with the Gnesio-Lutherans' confrontational "thus-says-the-Lord" approach, does stand in contrast to the more didactic style and its "come-let-us-reason-together" position of the Philippists—though the Philippists did write confessions on occasion and the Gnesio-Lutherans did write many books of instruction, using the commonplace method that Melanchthon had taught them at Wittenberg.[48]

Confession at the Papal Council

The Augsburg Confession had presented Lutheran teaching to the world in the political arena of the diet. At the same time, Melanchthon's confession took into account above all the theological and ecclesiastical-political positions of the Roman Catholic party. A confession to the world is also a confession to and for the church— for the confessors' supporters and opponents within the church.

The possibility of confessing before the church in a council arose in 1536, when Pope Paul III scheduled one for Mantua the following year. It did not actually begin meeting until 1545—and then in Trent. The Evangelical princes in Germany were invited to attend the scheduled council, so they gathered in the Hessian town of Smalcald in early 1537 to plan a strategy for confessing at the council. Luther had prepared an agenda for confessing at the papal council, the *Smalcald Articles*. The princes decided instead to use the text of the Augsburg Confession itself for their confession at the papal councils.

However, by 1551, when the opportunity for a Lutheran testimony before the papally-controlled assembly at Trent actually materialized, the Augsburg Confession was no longer deemed appropriate as an agenda for the Evangelical presentation. Two Lutheran confessions were composed for delivery at the Council of Trent in 1551, one by Melanchthon and his colleagues in Saxony, entitled "The Repetition of the Augsburg Confession," and the other by south German theologians who actually traveled to Trent as representatives of the duchy of Württemberg and the city of Strassburg.

Melanchthon wrote a preface for the Saxon confession when it was printed in 1552. In it he stated that the confession had not been composed to rekindle dissension in the church but rather to "recite simply and faithfully the summary of the teaching which is heard in all churches which embraced the confession of the Reverend Doctor Luther." The introductory paragraphs of the confession already stress the necessity of testifying against false teaching, error, and schism in spite of the dangers which arise from the hatred and lies of those embracing false teaching. Without such testimony generations to come will not know this truth. After a brief historical narrative tracing the current difficulties of the church back to the indulgence controversy of 1517 and after an overview of the controverted issues, the confession began its articles with a definition of the basis of divine teaching:

> Since it is most certain that God gathers His eternal church for Himself among the human race for the sake of His Son and through Him, through the speaking of the teaching which is written in the books of the prophets and the apostles, we affirm clearly ... that we embrace all the writings of the prophets and apostles in their intended sense, which is set forth in the Creeds—the Apostles', Nicene, and Athanasian.[49]

Melanchthon's understanding of doctrine and confession as verbal nouns, which bring the words of Scripture into action as believers speak them, is reflected in this confession of faith.

In south Germany the Swabian Lutheran theologians in the service of Duke Christoph of Württemberg—Johannes Brenz chief among them—prepared a confession that neighboring Strassburg also supported as an appropriate summary of Evangelical concerns to be presented to the council. It was published under the title *Confession,* but its introduction and conclusion say little about public testimony. Instead, they emphasize the necessity of "planning and preserving divine teaching." "Nothing," the confessors asserted, "is more useful and more pleasing to God for the edification and the preservation of the welfare of the church than the preaching of the divine Word and of true, pure teaching by government authorities and subjects." Reflecting Brenz's understanding of the relationship of church and state, the introduction of the confession states that rulers have an obligation to serve God and to support His church.

In line with this principle, the confession was presented as a report on the teaching and worship life of the churches of Württemberg, in which there was nothing that opposed the prophetic and apostolic Scriptures and the clear teaching of the true catholic church. This confession clearly states the need to condemn false teaching, but it lacks the spirit of sharp contention that soon marked the confessions of the Genesio-Lutheran party.[50] It reflects the attitude with which the Swabian theologians approached their participation in the papal council.

Toward a New Normative Confession

Apart from the call to this council by Pope Paul III, Melanchthon and his followers (and the Swabian Lutherans as well) found few occasions that required them to issue new confessions.[51] Instead, Philippists and Gnesio-Lutherans alike began to develop the *corpus doctrinae,* literally a *body of teaching,* a collection of confessional documents that were already published. These "bodies" were designed to regulate and define proper teaching within the church of a specific principality. Martin Chemnitz began an analysis of the controversies plaguing the Lutheran churches around 1560, with a chapter on the need for one *corpus doctrinae.* The purpose of such a body of teaching was to give proper form and an organized summary of the teaching of the Scriptures, which had been divinely restored through Luther's ministry, as this teaching had been expressed in the creeds tested by the church. Such a body of teaching would benefit the church, for it would provide a norm or standard of judgment so that cleverly disguised interpretations and obfuscations of the Biblical text could be rejected. If such standards are not in place in the church, Chemnitz observed, pure teaching will disappear. He cited the example of the Regensburg Colloquy of 1541, where artful compromises had led people astray from the purity of the Gospel. As a symbol, a proper form for teaching, Chemnitz recommended above all others the Augsburg Confession. To it he joined the Apology of the Confession and the Smalcald Articles. He argued for the inclusion of the latter because it treated several topics that the Augsburg Confession had omitted—"the papacy, the power of the bishops, Zwinglianism, transubstantiation, and sins which drive away the Holy Spirit."[52]

In 1560 such collections of confessions, whether entitled a *corpus doctrinae* or not, were issued by the electoral Saxon theologians, the so-called Corpus Philippicum, and by the ministeria of both Hamburg and Lübeck. Philippist bodies of teaching always included the Augsburg Confession and its Apology and usually contained Melanchthon's *Loci communes* or *Commonplaces* (topics) of Christian teaching, first published in 1521 and issued in revised editions after 1536. For the Gnesio-Lutherans the Smalcald Articles became a *sine qua non* for defining Lutheran doctrine in such bodies of teaching.[53]

119

The Gnesio-Lutheran Confessions

The first Gnesio-Lutheran confession had been issued at Magdeburg in 1550, in the midst of the Interims controversies, even before Melanchthon and the Swabians had prepared their new confessions for Trent. While the city was under siege by Moritz's imperial army, which wanted to eliminate the town's defiance of the Augsburg Interim, the Magdeburg ministerium published several defenses of the city's resistance to imperial religious policy. The pastors' *Confession* of April 13, 1550, placed this defense within the context of the *Hauptstücke* (chief parts) of Christian teaching. Nikolaus Gallus, who composed the confession, made it clear at the beginning of the document that the persecution unleashed by the papacy and the emperor in the Smalcald War and the attempts to enforce the Augsburg Interim had given occasion for this confession. He viewed his document as a continuation of the confession of Christian teaching which Luther and the confessors at Augsburg had delivered against "the Empire of the Antichrist."[54] The Magdeburg *Confession* might be considered the birth certificate of the Gnesio-Lutheran movement. It was the first of several confessional documents produced by members of the party.

In the midst of the controversies with their Philippist foes and others during the next quarter-century, the Gnesio-Lutherans found several occasions that demanded confession. One of these arose in Hamburg in 1557 when Joachim Westphal and his colleagues confessed their faith regarding the Lord's Supper against those who denied the real presence of Christ's body and blood in the bread and wine. This confession grew out of Westphal's persistent critique of Calvinistic conceptions of the Sacrament, which seemed to be spreading in Germany.[55]

The second of these confessional situations arose in ducal Saxony in 1559. There the ducal house issued its *Book of Confutation* as a confession of faith designed to end controversy within the Lutheran churches and to summon all Lutherans to unite against the errors that the ducal theologians perceived to be threatening the faith. John Frederick's two sons, Dukes John Frederick the Middler and John William, had decided to commission this *Book of Confutation* in the wake of two events: first, the disastrous breakup of the Evangelical negotiating team which met at imperial command to pursue doctrinal discussions with Roman Catholic theologians at Worms in 1557; and, second, the inadequate attempt of the Evangelical princes to forge Lutheran unity through the Frankfurt Recess of 1558. From their theological staff the princes initially chose Erhard Schnepf and the Philippists Viktorin Strigel and Andreas Hügel to produce such a document. The product of their deliberations did not please their Gnesio-Lutheran colleagues, Amsdorf, Flacius, and others. As a result, a group of Gnesio-Lutherans recast the document extensively. In that form it reviewed and rebutted the teachings of such Lutherans as Osiander, Stancarus, Major, the Adiaphorists, and the Antinomians; it likewise responded to the teachings of "radicals" such as Servetus, Schwenckfeld, Anabaptists, and Sacramentarians.[56]

Much the same concerns for guarding God's Word against sect and error moved the ministerium of the duchy of Mansfeld to formulate a document the same year. Under the leadership of two pastors, Superintendent Erasmus Sarcerius and Cyriakus Spangenberg (who shortly thereafter published the treatment of the need for Christian confession discussed above), the Mansfeld pastors also commented on and condemned the errors of those groups confuted in the Saxon *Book,* as well as the errors of Jesuits and "freewillers."[57]

The same set of concerns dominated the deliberations of theologians from the north German cities of Lübeck, Bremen, Hamburg, Rostock, Magdeburg, Braunschweig, Lüneburg, and Wismar in July 1561. The *Declaration* that their theologians signed at a meeting in Lüneburg also echoed the *Book of Confutation,* in part perhaps because the author of this Lüneburg *Declaration,* Joachim Mörlin (1514–71) of Braunschweig, had participated in the revision of the *Book.*[58] That same year internal turmoil over the Lord's Supper elicited a Confession on the Sacrament from the ministerium of the city of Bremen.[59]

By 1564 new intra-Evangelical tensions had arisen over the Lord's Supper and related teachings. The Mansfeld ministerium addressed a new confession to the relevant issues and errors and published it the following year.[60] In 1566 and 1567, from three widely-scattered parts of the Lutheran church and out of three different sets of circumstances, came four confessions issued by Gnesio-Lutherans. In Austria the Carinthian confession and the [Lower] Austrian confession were both composed in 1566 for presentation to the local estates to justify the proclamation of the Lutheran faith and to defend it against the attacks of papal foes.[61] In Antwerp Matthias Flacius, Cyriakus Spangenberg, and a small band of German preachers were assisting the local Lutheran congregation in organizing itself, and they produced for it an agenda and a confession. The purpose of the confession was to fix the doctrinal basis of the congregation's practice and to clarify the Lutheran sense of identity in the midst of the religious turbulence of this period of iconoclasm and clashes between more radical reformers and the Roman Catholic authorities.[62] In the small Saxon principalities ruled by the counts of Reuss (Greitz and Gerau) and Schönburg, the Gnesio-Lutherans were summoned to confess their teaching in the midst of local quarrels among princely brothers over the support of some of the Gnesio-Lutheran pastors in their realms.[63]

Each of these confessions claimed for itself a place in the line of succession begun at Augsburg in 1530. The Magdeburg *Confession* announced in its summary introduction that its first section was drawn from the Augsburg Confession, and the succeeding pages of the preface announced that it was doing battle against the Antichrist at Rome in the same way as had the third Elijah, Dr. Martin Luther, with the teaching set down at Augsburg only 20 years earlier.[64] The *Book of Confutation* claimed to continue the doctrine in the Augsburg Confession (in its original form), its Apology, and the Smalcald Articles—a list repeated in the *Declaration* of Lüneburg with the addition of Luther's catechisms.[65] The Antwerp *Confession* listed the *Book of Confutation* and the Mansfeld *Confession* of 1564 in addition to these as explications of Biblical teaching on which the faith of the subscribers rested. The *Confession* of Reuss and Schönburg included these and the Lüneburg *Declaration*, as well as Luther's writings in general, as authoritative documents.[66]

Changing Circumstances, Changing Mode of Confession

Although their authors perceived themselves to be writing in the train of confessors at Augsburg, their documents were different from the Augsburg document. The Augsburg Confession addressed its catholic appeal to catholic Christianity. In contrast, the *Confession* of Reuss and Schönburg, for instance, reflected the "remnant" ecclesiology and the defensive position of the Gnesio-Lutherans, who had experienced not merely nine years of condemnation from pope and emperor (as had the Augsburg confessors) but rather 30 to 45 years of persecutions of one kind or another.[67] The hopeful and confident note in the public confession at Augsburg had now turned defensive. From Magdeburg in 1550 to Antwerp and Reuss in 1567, these latter-day confessors recognized that the martyrdom of physical suffering and death may well come to those who give public witness to their faith. The Magdeburgers pledged themselves to follow the examples of the prophets, Christ, His apostles, and the ancient martyrs, for "it is God's own way of doing things that He leads us into suffering, the cross, and death under unjust force since He wants to conform us to the image of His Son."[68] The comrades of Flacius in Antwerp and their brethren in Reuss and Schönburg traced the line of those who had suffered for the truth back to Abel.[69] Cyriakus Spangenberg commented that the act of public confession had always provoked all sorts of danger, misfortune, and unrest for Christ's people, who live under Christ's Word—a Word of the cross—as He had promised in John 15 and 16. Spangenberg quoted John Hus to the effect that those who are least persecuted love other people more than they love the honor of God. Suffering produces sanctification.[70]

The Magdeburgers wrote their confession while their city was under siege from the electoral Saxon agents of Emperor Charles V. Hence they composed their confession in part to justify their armed resistance and that of their city government against imperial commands which, they believed, ran counter to both divine and natural law.[71] Other Gnesio-Lutheran confessions, also recognizing the fundamental principle that believers must obey God rather than man, therefore concluded that confessions may have to be issued in defiance of and in confrontation with governing authorities. Spangenberg argued that, although princes generally do not want the church to confess the faith, Christians must obey God's command to confess, as did Peter and John (Acts 4, Tob. 1), Daniel and the three men in the fiery furnace (Dan. 3 and 7), and the Maccabeans (2 Macc. 7).[72]

Caught in the tension between princely brothers in their counties, the confessors of Reuss and Schönburg tried to clarify their stance over against their rulers. The entire church of a land and its princes are not necessarily condemned when confessors of the Gospel point out that the princes are harboring one or two false teachers among them. It was not true, they insisted, that they were doing nothing in the pulpit but attacking princes or other theologians. On the other hand, Christ had commanded that they render Caesar his due and God His due (Matt. 22:21). They had to obey God rather than men (Acts 5:29). The examples of Christ and His apostles as well as that of Luther demonstrated that they had to stand up to rulers who opposed God's Word. They refused to purchase peace through silence and hypocrisy.[73]

Coupled with this adversarial posture towards rulers was an explicit eschatological understanding of the church. The Magdeburg *Confession* believed its confessing actions were set in the midst of that final battle between the Antichrist of Rome and God's third Elijah, Luther. This battle, they believed, was raging in Germany as the last mad charge of Satan against Christ and His church.[74] In 1559 the Mansfelders described their time as that in which Satan was once again creeping in to corrupt teaching, sacramental practice, worship, as well as the virtues, morality, and honor of those who had heard the truth. The Mansfeld confessors warned their readers to listen to Christ alone and to be as wise as serpents and as gentle as doves (Matt. 10:16) when examining all teaching and every teacher, because of Satan's wily striving always to deceive the people of God.[75]

A New Form for Confession

The Augsburg Confession set forth the articles of faith that summarized the Biblical teaching in a positive manner. It treated specific elements of Scriptural content and included within these articles condemnations of past heresies. The later addendum, the condemnation of heresy, took on special importance for the Gnesio-Lutherans,[76] and with the *Book of Confutation* they began to organize some of their confessions according to that structure. Instead of an overview of salient articles of faith, seven of these later confessions offered a review of specific heresies, heretical groups, or individuals—whether Lutheran, Reformed, Roman, or "radical" errorists (as noted in the summary of the *Book of Confutation* given above—although the Lüneburg *Declaration* did summarily treat certain basic teachings as well). Six articles examined the heresies and heretics whom they were refuting, using an outline that named the specific groups or individuals.

The Reuss-Schönburg confession treated the "heretical" groups under the outline of the six chief parts of Christian teaching in the Catechism. The four confessions under study that addressed a more catholic audience—those of Magdeburg in 1550 and of the Antwerp and the Carinthian and [Lower] Austrian Lutherans of 1566—were organized as general confessions of articles of faith. But the confessions of the ministeria of Hamburg (1557) and of Bremen (1561), which responded to the sacramentarian controversies, focused thematically on elements of dispute.

New Modes of Confession

These subsequent confessions differed from Augsburg in two other significant ways: *how* the confession was made and *who* made it. The Augsburg Confession had addressed its primary audience with *oral* confession and condemnation. As noted above, commentators viewed the Augsburg Confession first of all as a series of bold and daring acts, performed in word and deed throughout the spring and summer of 1530, climaxing in the reading of the document on June 25, 1530. None of these later documents was designed for oral delivery. Each recognized the effectiveness of the Augsburg Confession as a *document* and used the printed form of public witness. Nonetheless, reflecting the concerns of their colleague Cyriakus Spangenberg, the Mansfeld ministerium in its 1559 Confession insisted on the obligation of oral confession, and the confessors of Reuss and Schönburg also expressed their conviction that confession is fundamentally an oral activity and only secondarily written, even though their confession appeared in document form.[77]

The Augsburg Confession was made by the *princes,* through their spokesman, Christian Beyer. The confessions of the 1550s and 1560s bore the names of theologians—for the most part pastors rather than professors. Indeed, in 1564 the Mansfeld ministerium claimed that its right to confess was based upon its divine commission to care for the spiritual children of the clergy, who exercised the office of a spiritual paterfamilias over the people of the county.[78] This reflects in part the Gnesio-Lutheran conviction that the church must stand independent of the prince in all spiritual matters. It also reflects in part the changed situation of the Late Reformation. Confession had not been summoned to the public arena but rather arose within the church. Pastors, rather than princes, were being called to confess.

Nonetheless, the idea that God had also called lay people to confess their faith had not died out among these confessors. In 1567 the confession of Antwerp insisted that Baptism confers upon all baptized persons the call to confess God's name.[79] Among its subscribers was Cyriakus Spangenberg, who already seven years earlier had argued against those who would suggest that synods or the whole church of God alone should have power to condemn false teaching: "The common man does not act wrongly when he makes public confession against all new sects, in so far as this confession is informed by faith and is in accord with the rule of the Gospel and God's Word." This is not merely a privilege for every congregation and every Christian; it is a command from God to confess the faith and to confute error.[80] Spangenberg's ideal seems not to have captured the imaginations of his contemporaries. Of course, few lay people were in a position to compose a written confession, as, for example, Count Wolf von Schönburg did in the midst of the battles between the Gnesio-Lutherans and the Philippists.[81] But neither do we have indications that the clergy of the Late Reformation frequently encouraged their parishioners to confess their faith orally and publicly.

For a number of reasons the Gnesio-Lutheran clergy did recognize the need for their own confession. Some of their written confessions explain their purposes only briefly, probably assuming that the reason for confession was obvious. Others, for example the confessions of Mansfeld in 1559 and of [Lower] Austria in 1566, set forth extensive lists of reasons for public confession.

The Mansfeld Confession

The Mansfeld *Confession* began with the foremost purpose of any Christian confession: the honor of God. The Mansfelders continued with a series of purposes focusing on the chief concern of each of the confessions under study: the preservation of the purity of the teaching of the Word of God (the Gospel) against all error. The Mansfeld ministerium felt compelled to issue its confession because "we dare [not] close our eyes and let pure teaching collapse, with the result that we cannot be saved. For salvation is not to be found in lies and false teaching, is it?" Indeed, they viewed it as shameful to think that the pure teaching for which "our dear preceptors" had suffered "in these last times" should be permitted to disappear, since they had brought untold benefits for the whole church. Recognizing the need to oppose sects with both oral and written confessions, the Mansfeld ministerium did not want to rob their descendants of this pure teaching through their own lack of diligence.[82] This theme of promoting the pure teaching of Scripture and confuting false teachings of the sects was sounded in each of the confessions under study in much the same manner.[83] To these purposes the Mansfelders added their determination to continue the confession begun by the estates at Augsburg and their desire to receive God's reward and to avoid His punishment.[84]

The Austrian Confession

The [Lower] Austrian confession of 1566 developed a similar list of purposes for confessing the faith. Christians confess because that is the responsibility or office that God gives to all who trust in Him and because it is their trademark. Christians must give witness to their God and His Word as it is found in Scripture. Silence bears false witness in behalf of error. The Austrians further felt compelled to confront the papal party, which had accused them of teaching a secret doctrine which could not be brought into the open. Their confession was designed to demonstrate that they were teaching only what was contained in the the prophetic and apostolic Scriptures and in the unaltered Augsburg Confession, a defense both of their theological correctness and of their legality.

The Austrian Lutherans were also combatting the charge that they were divided among themselves. Their confession signaled their unity in faith and in worship practices. It was further intended to preserve their unity in the future, because it would build up the congregations of the Evangelical faith and confirm their adherents in a clarity of confession that embraced both teaching and worship. This confession would provide the governing authorities and their subjects with a written summary of the Christian faith and its true teaching so that they could judge teaching and distinguish the truth from lies and errors. It would call those who still lay in papal darkness to the true religion of Scripture, and it would encourage other

127

believers in Bohemia, Hungary, Gips, and Siebenburgen in their confession of the faith. The Austrians felt a special kinship in the faith for those fellow believers within and beyond Habsburg lands on both sides of the empire's southeastern border.[85]

Clearly, these lists of purposes or reasons for confession serve to emphasize that for these spokesmen, "confession" was more than just the documents they composed. Even though their statements were written rather than spoken, the confessors continued the understanding which the confessors at Augsburg certainly had: Confession is an act, far more than a document. The authors of these later confessions considered the documents to be instruments of the activity, function, and process of confessing, which could not be separated from the content conveyed by the writing of the documents. The purpose of the documents was to convey these three aspects—positively in the teaching of Scripture and negatively in the rejection of whatever opposed the Biblical teaching. The expression of the Reuss-Schönburg confessors, "we believe, teach, and confess" (also used in the Formula of Concord a decade later), illustrates, from the perspective of these theologians, how intertwined the action and significance of each of these verbs had become. Believing could not be separated from teaching and confessing.[86]

The object of the act of confessing is defined in various ways in these documents. Spangenberg offered his readers a catalog of definitions for the object of their confession: God's will, essence, Word, His Son and His Spirit, and His kingdom and His church.[87] The Gospel is frequently mentioned as the object of the confession of faith, as is divine truth;[88] but by far the most frequent is the verbal noun *teaching*. Teaching [*Lehre, doctrina*] comes in two forms: pure and false. Pure teaching comes from God, from Christ, and from God's Word, the apostolic and prophetic Holy Scriptures.[89] The pastors of Bremen affirmed,

> Our faith, understanding, and confession regarding the Holy Supper rest and are founded not on human reason or logical proofs from philosophy, but only upon the clear, plain Word of God, as recorded by the Evangelists Matthew, Mark, Luke, and by Paul. That this basis for faith stands sure and fast not only the Zwinglians but even the devil in hell must confess and concede. For . . . God

128

is truthful and reliable in all His words and is almighty and can do what He pleases.[90]

All of these confessions insisted, as would the Formula of Concord, that "the prophetic and apostolic writings of the Old and New Testaments" are the "pure and clear fountain of Israel, which is the only true norm according to which all teachers and teachings are to be judged and evaluated"; they used Holy Scripture as "the only judge, rule, and norm according to which as the only touchstone all teachings should and must be understood and judged as good or evil, right or wrong" (FC, Rule and Norm, SD 3, Ep. 7).

The pure *teaching* (doctrine) from Scripture is always stated in the singular. It is a body of teaching [*corpus doctrinae*].[91] False teaching is usually stated in the singular also, although on occasion reference may be made to false teachings (false systems of belief rather than specific elements of a single false system).[92] Confessors bestow a form [*forma*] upon the body of Biblical teaching.[93] This form takes shape in specific articles according to the situation in which confession is made, in the positive and negative statements of what is true and false, and in the language of the confession.[94] Pure teaching can be divided [*geteilt*], i.e, the "summary of teaching" may be comprehended in specific units or elements.[95] The church is called to confess these specific elements of the one body of God's teaching in specific situations, as well as against specific challenges to it. These specific elements may be labeled chapters [*Kapittel, capita*][96] or chief parts [*Heuptstücke*],[97] or—as in the Augsburg Confession—articles of faith.[98] Each of these terms refers to the elements of Biblical teaching in specific applications to a question raised regarding the meaning of Scripture as it addresses human life.

Particularly the Magdeburg *Confession* reveals how broadly the concept of Christian teaching might be cast. The Magdeburgers not only set forth chapters or chief parts on God, creation and sin, the Law and good works, the Gospel and justification, the holy sacraments, the church and the public ministry, but also on God's governance through the family and through the temporal authorities.[99] Involved as they were at that time in the Interims controversies, it is no wonder that the Magdeburgers also affirmed the inseparability of teaching from ceremonies. The Word, the sacraments, and public worship were of one piece for all these confessions, as can be seen clearly in the Mansfeld Confession of 1559.[100]

Confutation Is Inseparable from Confession

Each of the confessions under study made it clear, in their view, that the truth of God's Word could not be confessed apart from the confutation of error. In each case the occasion for a special act of confession was found not merely in the need to give witness to the faith, for that could take place in various kinds of documents. The invasion of Satan's forces in the form of sects and mobs—of errors and deceptions—drove each group of confessors to lift their voices through the printed page. The Gnesio-Lutherans in particular were convinced that the truth could not be confessed unless error was condemned, and they invented a new form for confession in the *Book of Confutation,* which took as its topics the errors of the foes of the truth rather than the positive articles of faith. Equally as dangerous as error, according to the Gnesio-Lutherans, who spoke on the basis of their experience with Melanchthon and his associates in the wake of the Augsburg Interim, was the refusal to confess by confronting error. Even many Lutherans had failed to support them in their confutation of the Interim and other errors. Such silence [*Stillschweigen*] was hypocrisy, a denial of the truth. Christians must confess.[101]

From Augsburg to the Formula of Concord

The Augsburg Confession had provided a pattern for a significant activity of the Christian life. It had legitimized lay participation in confession. It had used public confession as a means to proclaim and establish public dogma, and it became a test for the public teaching of the church. It had continued the ancient practice of confessing, both through the statement of positive belief and in the condemnation of error. A significant sector of the leadership of the Wittenberg movement in its second generation took this model seriously, both in theory and in practice. By the time the transition from the Reformation to Orthodoxy was being completed, the Lutheran church defined itself in terms of its public confession.

The Formula of Concord, as the concluding confession of this period of transition, demonstrates that the Lutheran confessors had continued in the tradition of the confessors at Augsburg, though they also deviated from their model in certain respects. It was now the *theologians* who made public confession of the faith, although they still did so at the behest of princes, who remained concerned about the public confession of the church both for reasons of public policy and their own personal faith. Therefore, in the case of the Formula of Concord, the princes claimed the right to subscribe the new formula of confession publicly along with their theologians.

The "formulators" were not innovators. They followed the model of the ancient church, which had frequently condemned false teaching and regarded confrontation as an aspect of confession. The formulators are sometimes criticized for fostering a narrow vision of the church, as though they chose to isolate themselves from those who did not agree with them; but that charge is only partially justified. Theirs was an ecumenical vision. They continued to believe that the truth of the Gospel must be shared broadly. But unfortunately, the division of Christendom into new groups based on "confessions," which began after Augsburg, had progressed so far by the end of the 16th century that the formulators faced new fronts and new issues that continued to require defending the faith rather than seeking organizational unification. What should be noted is that Germany in the 16th century was merely a geographic expression referring to numerous individual political states. Therefore the very gathering of German territorial *churches* into one common confession of faith was in itself, as Ernst Koch has pointed out, an ecumenical accomplishment of great significance for its time.[102]

The world changed and so did the churches of western Europe during the course of the half century after the Augsburg Confession. As the divisions between confessional groups hardened—in part by persecution and religious war—the sense of defensiveness in each of these groups rose. Even though the joyful and confident spirit of Augsburg had become somewhat muted in this new situation, the German Lutherans during this period continued to define what it meant to be Christian in the same way: God's Word had to be confessed. The church would remain faithful to its God-given assignment and demand only if it continued to preach the Gospel in conformity with a pure understanding of it and administered the sacraments in accordance with the divine Word.

131

5

Confessing the Faith As a Way of Life

Confessional—Lutherans use the word in a fashion unique in Christendom. We do not speak of "confessional Roman Catholic," or "confessional Greek Orthodox," or even "confessional Calvinist," and certainly not "confessional fundamentalist"—even though in Europe Roman Catholicism is called a "confession" and the Calvinists have more confessional documents than the Lutherans do.

To be confessional points to the essence of what Lutherans in the 16th century defined their cause to be. The Lutheran church may have been conceived in the university, in Martin Luther's personal struggle and in his professional study of Holy Scripture for the lecture hall; but the Lutheran church was born in the public forum as princes and municipal representatives stood before their emperor and their world with a bold and forthright confession of their faith. This confession has been regarded by Lutherans ever since as the chief symbol of what they are about as God's people.

The Need for Secondary Authority

Whether Christians realize and acknowledge it or not, everyone uses principles of interpretation, because the Scriptures (read by themselves without guidelines) too easily can overwhelm the individual. The enthusiastic spirit within all believers can wrest any passage from its Biblical context and place it in the setting of one's own inevitable (though perhaps unrecognized) cultural prejudices. In part to check this predilection, the 16th-century Lutheran confessors chose three ancient creeds and seven similar contemporary documents as their secondary authorities. They labeled them *confessions*—statements growing out of their experiences in bringing the Word of God to bear on life in their culture in the wake of Augsburg.

132

Some Christians may deceive themselves into thinking that they operate without such secondary authorities, written or unwritten, of one kind or another, but they do not. The medieval church had its popes and councils, and the independent Bible church founded yesterday has its principles—perhaps not organized or articulated—which were and are prepared to adjudicate disputes in which passages of Scripture could be cited against each other. All Christians have a court of appeals to which they turn when conflicting interpretations of a single Bible passage confront them, even though individual believers may not be able to identify the secondary authority to which they would turn in advance of the necessity of doing so. Thus, when Lutherans pledged themselves to their creeds and confessions, they were only making clear where they would turn for this kind of adjudication, interpretation, and guidance in the theological tasks of the church. They were forthrightly identifying how the authority of the inspired Scriptures moves into the life of the church.

Some Lutherans have been confused about what it means to be confessional. It does not mean, for example, simply claiming a certain historical tradition in name while ignoring it in the daily practice of the church. It does not mean viewing the Lutheran confessional documents as ends in themselves. Too often Lutherans have faltered into a kind of confessional*ism* that seeks identity, security, and meaning by holding on to the confessional documents rather than continuing to confess their content, speaking of their Lord and His forgiving love. The spirit of the Augsburg Confession is not reflected with a siege mentality; that seems to make the working of God's Gospel dependent on the church and its defense of the confessional documents. The spirit of Augsburg is best reflected in the song of the freeing power of the Gospel of Jesus Christ. His Gospel liberates His people to sing even in the midst of a world bent on fostering the siege mentality and, with it, the defeat of God's people.

When and Where to Confess

Most Lutherans today do not venture into the halls of Congress with their confession as the first Lutheran confessors did at Augsburg. Yet Christians in the late 20th century do encounter occasions in every phase of life that call for confession. At work and at home, in the neighborhood, school, club, and recreational center—as well as more overtly in the congregation of God's people—such situations arise. When those around them ask questions—whether inquiring or challenging—which the living voice of the Gospel can meet, the spirit of Augsburg leads the heirs of Elector John and Landgrave Philip, of Luther, Bugenhagen, and Melanchthon, to point in appropriate form and detail to the Biblical message.

Lutherans in the 16th century believed that God uses human language not only to provide signposts pointing to a heavenly reality but also to express His power to kill and make alive. Out of this conviction arose their belief that the faith must be confessed publicly. They believed that the Word continues to exercise its power as believers take the Word from the pages of Scripture to apply and confess it in specific situations. Therefore, they were able to select certain public confessions to serve as secondary authorities in the church because those confessions faithfully reflected the content of the Biblical message. These Lutheran confessors believed that every individual Christian is called to interpret Scripture, but they also believed that individual Christians need the support and counsel of each other as they bring God's Word from Bible to hearers. Thus, like all Christians, they used secondary authority to guide them in their individual interpretation and confession of the faith.

Sometimes this confession will come quite directly from the Lutheran Confessions. Very often it will come directly from Scripture instead, because some of the questions of the late 20th century are not those once encountered by 16th-century Christians. In both cases, if the answers are the true responses to the spiritual needs of the day, they will come from God's Word in Holy Scripture. Moreover, even when the Confessions do not speak explicitly to the questions of today, they will guide the formulation of answers by highlighting the well-worn channels of Biblical confession, always centered in God's action in Jesus Christ and His care for His people through the Holy Spirit. On this bedrock of truth—not on delight in the action of confessing or on any other human feeling—the confession is given. On this bedrock its effectiveness rests.

Some Lutherans may wonder what to do about the many current questions which, because of different circumstances, the Lutheran Confessions did not and could not address directly. They may wonder whether it is time for a new confession. That cannot be decided with certainty. Christians, individually and collectively, go about their calling, confessing their faith, trusting that the Lord of His church will lead the church to determine when a new form is needed or a specific form of confession merits special status that should be recognized as authoritative for the church's proclamation and life—subject, of course, to the Scriptures. Consciously distinguishing between Biblical truth, on the one hand, and the application or meaning of that truth for the problems of the day, on the other hand, God's people need not worry as long as they are engaged in faithful confession of the faith.

Confessing the One True Evangel

The confessors at Augsburg recognized that faith in Jesus Christ has many implications, and it is important for believers to confess the fullness of the message about Him. There is only one Evangel. *The* Gospel is not just any good news for a bad situation, any good news that fosters good feelings or attains a desired result in terms of human action. Confessing the Christian faith is naming the name which is above every name, and doing so on bended knee. Confessing the Christian faith is naming the name apart from which there is no salvation. Confessing the Christian faith is confessing Jesus Christ and all that Scripture says about God who had come among us in human flesh.

Those Lutherans at Augsburg set a model for their followers first of all with regard to their understanding of the content of the Scriptures. That content is God's Word of Law and Gospel—above all His Evangel, the Good News of His love for fallen sinners in Jesus Christ. The Lutheran confession of the faith is permeated by God's historical revelation of Himself in Jesus of Nazareth. The Creator God—the God of Abraham, Isaac, and Jacob, the God who became flesh and dwelt among us as Jesus Christ—is the subject of their confession. Within the conceptual framework of the Biblical writers, their trust in Him and their confession of His name brings light and life to those whom the Holy Spirit has brought to depend on it.

The Lutheran confessors of the 16th century, like most people in most cultures, remained unburdened by modern ideas of the multiplicity or complexity of truth. Today's confessors are confronted by the suggestion—or, more correctly, by the assumption—that truth is relative and multiform. No one, of course, believes that all claims are equal regarding matters of ultimate concern. Even rank relativists and pluralists refuse to compromise certain "self-evident" truths. But, like their predecessors at Augsburg, contemporary Lutherans insist that what they confess is a statement of the truth relating to ultimate human reality. Their concept of truth is centered in God who entered time and space, fashioning Himself in one truly human image, that of Jesus of Nazareth.

Part of what Luther and Melanchthon understood in structuring their confession of faith was that the *articles* or topics of the faith (as found, for example, in the Augsburg Confession) are not so many equally valuable pearls on a string, with so many required to make the string a necklace and so many dispensable. Instead, they believed that Biblical teaching is like a human body. Christ is its head; decapitated it dies. When the arm of Baptism is cut off, or the foot of eschatology badly mangled, the whole body suffers. It can survive with serious injury, but it may also hemorrhage and bleed to death. Believers use their opportunities for confession to keep the whole body of Biblical teaching healthy, both in its faithfulness to the Biblical Word and in its apt communication to the people who need to hear it.

In a world of sin, eventually confession of the truth also leads to confrontation with human attempts to refashion God in human images. Some formulations of God's message for His people are right, and some are wrong. In this world the church must still wrestle with the father of lies. Deceiving forms of religion, within and outside the church, are always trying to restrain the power of God's Word. Therefore the church's confession of faith must exclude deceivers as at the same time it invites and includes those whom the Holy Spirit opens to His Word. Neither God nor His Word takes to leashes. All human attempts to redesign the hidden God to fit preferred human forms not only fail but also deceive and kill. They must be opposed. In the midst of such deceit the confession of God's Word comes to bring a sword, not peace. The Lutheran confessors were convinced that that sword was a surgical sword, meant ultimately not for the destruction of those deceiving or being deceived, but of deceit itself.

The sword of confession is two-edged. It is also the scalpel of the healing and forgiving truth of the Gospel of Jesus Christ. There-fore, *it must be wielded with utmost care and with obvious love and concern.* If condemnation does not spring from love for those caught in untruth, and if it is not effective in combating untruth, then it is improper condemnation. Confessing the faith opposes whatever subverts the faith. It never does so for the sake of defending our own persons but rather for the sake of bringing others to Christ and preserving them in the faith. Confessors thus must listen to themselves through the ears of their hearers to make certain their condemnation is clearly understood as an agent of God's truth, not of the confessor's defensiveness or private agenda.

In the 20th-century West, condemnation almost always will have to be more gentle and respectful than it frequently was in the 16th century. It dare not be less clear and direct, but must be motivated more obviously by love for the confused or erring. For only when it sounds a loving call for repentance will our condemnation please God. Only when it is not done as our own good work, to make us look good in His sight, but to win the erring brother or sister, will it fulfill God's purposes.

Confessing Ecumenically

Because they saw themselves as servants of the life-giving Word, the Lutherans of the 16th century pledged themselves to proclaim the Evangel of Jesus Christ. In so doing they pledged themselves to be both evangelistic and ecumenical as God's eschaton approached.

The confessors could not help but speak of what they had heard and seen. They could not fail to engage all Christians in conversation, especially those who were erring, so that they could give witness to their faith—and in so doing they laid themselves open to ad-monitions regarding their own expression of the Biblical message.

It is impossible to live in the spirit of Augsburg and not be determinedly ecumenical. This spirit soberly assesses the realities of the struggle between the Gospel itself and the cultures in which the Gospel is confessed. This spirit practices daily the repentance that is not only the whole life of individual believers but also of the institutional church. It refuses to let itself or other groups of Chris-tians off the hook with regard to the need to repent for having subverted the Gospel through cultural biases. This spirit never ignores its own need and the need of others to return daily to a proper and salutary confession of the faith. If Christians discover that their mode of calling one another to repentance for error in confession is preventing a proper hearing of their message, they are compelled to alter their mode of condemnation. Condemnation will inevitably and necessarily offend those who are living comfortably apart from God's truth. But Christians will make certain that the offense comes from confrontation with God's Word—from Christ's cross—and that offense has not been *given* by their own defensiveness, boorishness, or attempts at self-justification. The goal, when judging and rejecting false understandings of human life and of God's Word, is to lead sinners to abandon false belief, not to make us feel good about ourselves.

The ecumenical concern of those at Augsburg is seen in their determined effort to remain in dialog with their opponents and to persuade them of the truth of the Lutheran confession of the faith. At Augsburg Melanchthon and his colleagues demonstrated great patience and perseverance. This marked their confession after the diet as well (e.g., in the successful effort of negotiating the Wittenberg Concord on the Lord's Supper with the south Germans). The spirit of Augsburg calls on Christians to confess to one another, so that together all may return to the Biblical message, so that they may give faithful witness to that message and its author alongside each other.

Confessing Evangelistically

The spirit of Augsburg is also determinedly evangelistic. Those first Lutherans were certain that the content of such a message could not remain a secret. They knew that it is a contradiction in terms to tell a child a secret, and they believed that they were first of all children of God. They knew that to be a "confessional" Lutheran they must not only clutch documents to their hearts, they must also be confessing the faith to people who need to hear it. For *confessional* is a verbal adjective. It describes a commitment to the God who has committed Himself to His people with His promise, a commitment to respond by confessing the utter reliability of the promise and the Promiser.

Those first Lutheran confessors were both lay and clergy. Their movement, as noted above, had been born in the university, and their confession relied on the best theological thinking at hand. Their confession was not carelessly thrown together but carefully crafted through rigorous intellectual labor. However, the labor of the theological minds, both lay and clergy, was put at the disposal of all believers. Lay believers had been called on to confess at Augsburg, and these first Lutheran confessors boldly and gladly risked the sacrifices that threatened them when they stood before their emperor, the enemy of their faith, and made open confession. God calls lay people and pastors alike to such ecumenical and evangelistic confession. The confessors at Augsburg recognized the differences as well as the similarities in the calling and the role of the pastor and of the lay person. They recognized that both are called by God to spread His Word of life and peace. They confessed that Christ has called all baptized believers to confess His name, and they knew that trust in the heart produces confession with the lips. They recognized that pastors and congregations are not rivals, bound to be fighting over a proper division of power, but are instead part of one body, both dedicated to using the power of God's Word in specific ways for confessing the faith. In witnessing to God's Word, the confessors at Augsburg and their heirs in the era of the Interims were also conscious that confession of the faith involves more than just "doctrine"—more than just the words which convey God's Word. The practice of the church—its liturgy and hymns, its public symbols and activities—also contributes to what people perceive and understand by "presenting the Gospel." Confessors must be sensitive to the dynamics of the wide range of human perceptions as they encounter the confession of the faith in all its many facets, realizing that each person has different presuppositions and understandings that have emerged from his personal social background.

Confessors need daily assistance in formulating the Word of God in oral form for their hearers. The Lutheran Confessions provide structures and formulations for loosing the truth and power of God's Word. Therefore, they provide the secondary authority for the church's life, an authority which gives life because it repeats faithfully what the Scriptures say. Confessors also remember their own need to repent daily—for personal sins, to be sure, but especially for not being as winsome as they might be, for missing opportunities, for not always being understanding and patient, or for not showing the courage that God expects.

Lutheran witnesses who are drawing unbelievers to faith in Jesus Christ will find in the Lutheran Confessions significant resources for their own evangelistic activity. In the Confessions, particularly from the catechisms, they will find guidance for how God uses His human instruments in bringing the Gospel to others and they will find texts to use in instructing those outside the faith in its content.

Confessing Eschatologically

As they gave witness to the Gospel, the confessors at Augsburg believed they were not only standing before emperor, empire, and world, but also before God. Theirs was, they were convinced, an eschatological moment. They believed that God's judgment was hanging over an apostate Christendom and that the last day would not be delayed long. For this reason they felt an urgency to confess, but they also set forth their confession with a strong confidence in the power of God's Word and a joyful hope that He would stand by them and let His Word take proper course.

All Christians, including Lutherans, have some sense of the eschatological urgency of their confessions. They can see and sense the signs of God's wrath against apostasy and immorality in their own societies. Instead of greeting these signs with self-serving defensiveness or mere wails of complaint, they rejoice in the sharpened opportunities which such signs of His wrath give them to speak of His Gospel to neighbors and friends whose lives are not holding together under new stresses and strains. As they sense the signs of judgment over their own cultures, they recognize God's call to witness to His love in Jesus Christ with joy and hope, with confidence in the power that lies in the Word that they confess, under the shadow of His approaching day. Doing so, they reaffirm the identity that the confessors at Augsburg claimed for themselves and those who followed after them.

For them and for their heirs, confessing Jesus Christ and His unconditional Gospel is *the* way of life.

Appendix A

The Chronology of Lutheran Confession in the Sixteenth Century

	EVENTS	CONFESSIONAL DOCUMENTS
1517	Luther posts the Ninety-five Theses	
1524–1525	The controversy between Luther and Erasmus	
1528		Luther's *Confession Concerning Christ's Supper*
1529		Luther's Catechisms
1530		The Augsburg Confession
1531		The Apology of the Augsburg Confession
1537		The Smalcald Articles
1546	Luther's death	
1546–1547	The Smalcald War	
1548	The Augsburg Interim and the Leipzig Interim	
1550		The Magdeburg Confession
1551		The Saxon Repetition of the Augsburg Confession
1551		The Württemberg Confession
1557		The Hamburg Confession
1559		The Saxon Book of Confutation
1559		The First Mansfeld Confession

1561		The Lüneburg Declaration
1561		The Bremen Confession
1564		The Second Mansfeld Confession
1566		The Carinthian Confession
1566		The (Lower) Austrian Confession
1567		The Antwerp Confession
1567		The Reuss-Schönburg Confession
1568–1570	Jakob Andreae's first attempt to formulate Lutheran concord	
1573–1577	Efforts toward the Formula of Concord	
1577		The Formula of Concord
1580		The Book of Concord

Appendix B

Articles of Faith of Selected Confessions

I. THE AUGSBURG CONFESSION (1530)

1. God
2. Original Sin
3. The Son of God
4. Justification
5. The Office of the Ministry and the Means of Grace
6. New Obedience
7. The Church
8. What the Church Is
9. Baptism
10. The Holy Supper of Our Lord
11. Confession and Absolution
12. Repentance
13. The Use of the Sacraments
14. Order in the Church
15. Church Usages
16. Civil Government
17. The Return of Christ to Judgment
18. Freedom of the Will
19. The Cause of Sin
20. Faith and Good Works
21. The Cult of Saints

[Articles on issues of reform:]
22. Both Kinds in the Sacrament
23. The Marriage of Priests
24. The Mass
25. Confession and Absolution
26. The Distinction of Foods
27. Monastic Vows
28. The Power of Bishops

II. THE SMALCALD ARTICLES (1537)

Part One: The Triune God
Part Two: The Office and Work of Jesus Christ, or Our Redemption
   1. Christ and Faith
   2. The Mass (including the Invocation of Saints)
   3. Chapters and Monasteries
   4. The Papacy
Part Three: Discussable Articles

1. Sin
2. The Law
3. Repentance
4. The Means of the Gospel
5. Baptism
6. The Sacrament of the Altar
7. The Keys
8. Confession and Absolution
9. Excommunication
10. Ordination and Vocation
11. The Marriage of Priests
12. The Church
13. How the Human Creature Is Justified before God, and Good Works
14. Monastic Vows
15. Human Traditions

III. THE REPETITION OF THE AUGSBURG CONFESSION (1551)

[Articles in the German version which do not occur as separate articles in the Latin version are given in parentheses]
1. Doctrine
2. The Trinity [and the Cause of Sin]
3. Original Sin
4. The Remission of Sins and Justification
    (What the Word *Faith* Means)
    (What *To Be Justified* Means)
5. The Free Will [absent as a separate article in the German]
6. New Obedience
7. Those Works Which Are Required
8. How Good Works Can Be Done
9. How New Obedience Pleases God
10. Rewards
11. The Distinction between Sins [absent as a separate article in the German]
12. The Church
    (What the Christian Church Is)
    (What the False Church Is)
    (Marks of the True Church of God)
    (The Distinction of the Church from Civil Government)
    (On Ordination and the Glory of the Ministry or Preaching Office)
13. The Sacraments
14. Baptism
15. The Lord's Supper
    (Sacrifice)

16. Repentance
17. Satisfaction
18. Marriage
19. Confirmation and Extreme Unction
20. Ceremonies
21. The Monastic Life
22. The Invocation of the Pious, Who Have Departed This Life
23. Civil Government

IV. THE MAGDEBURG CONFESSION (1550)

1. God, and the Distinction of the Persons in the Divine Essence
2. Creation and Sin, Whence Sin Comes, and What It Is
3. The Law and Good Works
4. The Gospel and Justification
5. The Holy Sacraments
6. The Church and Ministers of the Church and Their Power
7. Temporal Governance and the Governance of the Household and Their Power

V. THE SAXON BOOK OF CONFUTATION (1559)

1. Servetus
2. Schwenckfeld
3. The Antinomians
4. The Anabaptists
5. The Sacramentarians
6. The Free Will
7. Osiander and Stancarus
8. Dr. Major
9. The Adiaphorists

VI. THE FIRST MANSFELD CONFESSION (1559)

1. The Anabaptists
2. The Followers of [Michael] Servetus
3. The Followers of Stancarus
4. The Jesuits
5. The Antinomians
6. The Schwenckfelder
7. The Zwinglians or Sacramentarians
8. The Osiandrians
9. Those Who Misuse the Doctrine of the Free Will

10. Those Who Have Brought Back the Papistic Expression "Good Works Are Necessary for Salvation" in These Times
11. Those Who Have Wanted to Act in Weakness in Regard to Adiaphora

VII. THE LÜNEBURG DECLARATION (1561)

Part One: The Form of Teaching
Part Two:
    1. Osiandrists
    2. Majorists
    3. Sacramentarians
    4. Adiaphorists
    5. Synergists or the Free Will

VIII. THE SECOND MANSFELD CONFESSION (1564)

1. Dr. Paul Eber's Book [on the Lord's Supper]
2. The Errors of the Heidelberg Catechism
3. The Ascension of Christ into Heaven
4. Dr. Georg Major's Preface
5. The Revived Antinomianism of Johann Agricola of Eisleben
6. On Synergism and the Errors of Victorin Strigel

IX. THE CARINTHIAN CONFESSION (1566)

1. The Law—Sorrow or Repentance
2. The Gospel—Faith or the Gracious Forgiveness of Sins
3. The Sacraments
4. The Mass
5. New Obedience or the Good Works of the Children of God
6. The Head of the Church
7. The Calling and Conduct of Ministers of the Church

X. THE (LOWER) AUSTRIAN CONFESSION (1566)

1. The Holy Scripture
2. The Writings of the Dear Fathers and Also of the Teachers, Who Serve the Church with Their Writings in Our Own Time

3. God
4. The Human Creature
5. Law and Gospel
6. Repentance
7. Faith in Christ
8. The Justification of the Human Creature before God
9. Good Works
   Prayer
   The Veneration of Dead Saints
   Fasting
   Alms
10. The Sacraments
11. Holy Baptism
12. The Holy Supper of Christ
13. The Mass
14. The Power of the Keys
    Absolution
    Excommunication
15. The Church
16. The Communion of Saints
17. The Resurrection of the Dead
18. Eternal Life
19. The Calling and Conduct of Preachers
20. The Marriage of Priests
21. The Pope's Authority and Power
22. The Property of the Church
23. Temporal Authority
24. The Obedience of Subjects to Governing Authorities
25. Usury
26. Worship Services
27. Ceremonies or Adiaphora

XI. THE ANTWERP CONFESSION (1567)

1. The Norm of Truth
2. God
3. Original Sin and Freedom of the Will
4. The Incarnation of God's Son and the Redemption of the Human Creature

XII. The Formula of Concord (1577)

Notes

Chapter 1: Confessing Christ from Augsburg to the Nations

1. Hermann Sasse, *Here We Stand: Nature and Character of the Lutheran Faith,* trans. Theodore G. Tappert (1938; reprint, St. Louis: Concordia, n.d.), 91.
2. David P. Daniel and Charles P. Arand, *A Bibliography of the Lutheran Confessions* (*Sixteenth Century Bibliography* 28; St. Louis: Center for Reformation Research, 1988) offers a thorough bibliographical overview of the subject.

   The 450th anniversary of the presentation of the Augsburg Confession produced a host of commemorative volumes and celebrations. Even before this anniversary, the Augsburg Confession had become a focus for ecumenical discussion. See, among many other volumes, *Katholische Anerkennung des Augsburgischen Bekenntnisses* (Frankfurt/M: Lembeck, 1977), translated as *The Role of the Augsburg Confession: Catholic and Lutheran Views,* ed. Joseph A. Burgess (Philadelphia: Fortress, 1980); *Die Confessio Augustana im ökumenischen Gespräch,* ed. Fritz Hoffmann and Ulrich Kuhn (Berlin: Evangelische Verlagsanstalt, 1980); see also the comments of Friedrich Wilhelm Kantzenbach, *Augsburg 1530–1580: Ökumenisch-europäische Perspektiven* (Munich: Kaiser, 1979) on the significance of the Confession for Europe today, esp. 9–21. Out of these discussions came the volume *Confessio Augustana: Bekenntnis des einen Glaubens* (Frankfurt/M: Lembeck, and Paderborn: Bonifacius-Druckerei, 1980), translated as *Confessing One Faith: A Joint Commentary on the Augsburg Confession by Lutheran and Catholic Theologians,* ed. George W. Forell and James F. McCue (Minneapolis: Augsburg, 1982).

   On the role the Augsburg Confession and the other Lutheran confessional writings play in Lutheran churches, see *The Church and the Confessions: The Role of the Confessions in the Life and Doctrine of the Lutheran Churches,* ed. Vilmos Vajta and Hans Weissgerber (Philadelphia: Fortress, 1963); and, e.g., *Zur bleibenden Aktualität des Augsburger Bekenntnisses,* ed. Gottfried Klapper (Fuldaer Hefte 25; Hamburg: Lutherisches Verlagshaus, 1981).

   Still of great help to English-speaking students of the Augsburg Confession is J. Michael Reu, *The Augsburg Confession: A Collection of Sources with an Historical Introduction* (Chicago: Wartburg, 1930; reprint, St. Louis: Concordia, 1983).

   An excellent overview of the non-religious aspects of the Diet of Augsburg is found in Gottfried G. Krodel, "Law, Order, and the Almighty *Taler*: The Empire in Action at the 1530 Diet of Augsburg," *The Sixteenth Century Journal* XIII, 2 (1982): 75–106.
3. Werner Elert, "Der Weg zum kirchlichen Bekenntnis: Zum Augustana-Jubiläum 1930," *Ein Lehrer der Kirche, Kirchlich-theologische Aufsätze und Vorträge von*

Werner Elert, ed. Max Keller-Hüschemenger (Berlin: Lutherisches Verlagshaus, 1967), 92–93.

4. Ibid.

5. Arthur C. Cochrane, "The Act of Confession-Confessing," in *Formula of Concord: Quadricentennial Essays; The Sixteenth Century Journal* VIII, 4 (1977): 61.

6. Gunter Lanczkowski, "Glaubensbekenntnis(se) I. Religions-geschichtlich," *Theologische Realenzyklopädie,* Gerhard Krause and Gerhard Muller, eds. (Berlin/New York: de Gruyter, 1977–), 13:384–85.

7. Hans Schwarz, "Glaubensbekenntnis(se) IX. Dogmatisch," ibid., 437–40.

8. Henning Schroer, "Glaubensbekenntnis(se) X. Praktisch-theologisch," ibid., 442.

9. Regin Prenter, *Das Bekenntnis von Augsburg: Eine Auslegung* (Erlangen: Martin Luther, 1980), 9.

10. Erich Vogelsang, "Der Confessio-Begriff des jungen Luther (1513–1522)," *Luther-Jahrbuch* XII (1930): 94, (91–108).

11. Erhard S. Gerstenberger, "Glaubensbekenntnis(se) II. Altes Testament," *Theologische Realenzyklopädie,* 13:386–88, and Klaus Wengst, "Glaubensbekenntnis(se) IV. Neues Testament," ibid., 392–99. Wilhelm Andersen, "Die Notwendigkeit einer Entfaltung des christlichen Glaubensbekenntnisses und die Problematik einer detaillierten begrifflichen Festlegung," in *Vom Dissensus zum Konsensus, Die Formula Concordiae von 1577* (Hamburg: Lutherisches Verlagshaus, 1980), 113–45. On the earliest Christian confessions, see Fred Danker, *Creeds in the Bible* (St. Louis: Concordia, 1966); Oscar Cullmann, *The Earliest Christian Confessions,* trans. J. K. S. Reid (London: Lutterworth, 1949); and J. N. D. Kelly, *Early Christian Creeds* (New York: McKay, 1960).

12. Friedrich Wilhelm Kantzenbach, "Aspekte zum Bekenntnisproblem in der Theologie Luthers," *Luther-Jahrbuch* 1963, 70, 72–73. These are his observations on Luther's understanding of confessing the faith.

13. Joachim Staedtke, "Bekenntnis und Kirche aus reformierter Sicht," in *Kirche und Bekenntnis: Historische und theologische Aspekte zur Frage der gegenseitigen Anerkennung der lutherischen und der katholischen Kirche auf der Grundlage der Confessio Augustana,* ed. Peter Meinhold (Wiesbaden: Steiner, 1980), 58, 59.

14. Jörg Baur, "Historische und systematische Erwägungen zum Problem des Bekenntnisses. Die Einwände des neuzeitlichen Bewusstseins gegen 'das Statuarische in der Religion'," in *Vom Dissensus zum Konsensus,* 62–66.

15. Ibid., 61–62.

16. Arthur C. Cochrane, "The Act of Confession-Confessing," 77, summarizes the arguments of the Formula of Concord for the necessity of condemnation. See also Hans-Werner Gensichen, *We Condemn: How Luther and 16th-Century Lutheranism Condemned False Doctrine,* trans. Herbert J. A. Bouman (St. Louis: Concordia, 1967). In regard to the Augsburg Confession, see Wilhelm Maurer, *Historischer Kommentar zur Confessio Augustana,* 2 vols. (Gütersloh: Mohn, 1976, 1978), 1:61–70; translated as *Historical Commentary on the Augsburg Confession,* trans. H. George Anderson (Philadelphia: Fortress, 1986), 48–57.

17. Armin-Ernst Buchrucker, "Einheit im Bekenntnis der Wahrheit: Von Sinn, Ziel

und Problematik der Konkordienformel," in *Bekenntnis zur Wahrheit: Aufsätze über die Konkordienformel,* ed. Jobst Schöne (Erlangen: Martin Luther, 1978), 20.

18. *Deutsches Wörterbuch,* ed. Jacob Grimm and Wilhelm Grimm, I (Leipzig: Hirzel, 1854), 1417.

19. Cited in Heinrich Schmid, *Doctrinal Theology of the Evangelical Lutheran Church,* 3rd ed., trans. Charles A. Hay and Henry E. Jacobs (1875; reprint, Minneapolis: Augsburg, 1961), 101–2.

20. For example, on the differences between the Lutheran and the Reformed view of formal confessions, see Sasse, *Here We Stand,* 97–108; Staedtke, *Kirche und Bekenntnis,* and Hans Jörg Urban, "Die Gültigkeit der Reformatorischen Bekenntnisse Heute," *Catholica* (1977): 169–201, esp. 181–201.

21. Ernst Walter Zeeden, *Die Entstehung der Konfessionen: Grundlagen und Formen der Konfessionsbildung im Zeitalter der Glaubenskämpfe* (Munich: Oldenbourg, 1965).

22. Ibid., 7–10, 32–34.

23. Clearly, the theology of Lutheran Orthodoxy remained largely faithful to the Lutheran Confessions. But the actual use and citation of the confessional documents was more limited. See, in the case of the Formula of Concord, Robert D. Preus, "The Influence of the Formula of Concord on the Later Lutheran Orthodoxy," in *Discord, Dialogue, and Concord: Studies in the Lutheran Reformation's Formula of Concord,* ed. Lewis W. Spitz and Wenzel Lohff (Philadelphia: Fortress, 1977), 86–101. On *The Book of Concord* as a whole, see Johannes Wallmann, "Die Rolle der Bekenntnisschriften im älteren Luthertum," in *Bekenntnis und Einheit der Kirche: Studien zum Konkordienbuch,* ed. Martin Brecht and Reinhard Schwarz (Stuttgart: Calwer, 1980), 381–92. J. A. O. Preus has shown that this generalization cannot be applied to Martin Chemnitz, who did cite the Augsburg Confession, for example, in his *Fundamenta sanae doctrinae de vera et substantiali praesentia, exhibitione & sumptione corporis & sanguinis Domini in Coena* (Jena: Richtzenhan, 1590); translated as *The Lord's Supper,* trans. J. A. O. Preus (St. Louis: Concordia, 1979), 21–22.

24. Heinz Schilling, "Die Konfessionalisierung im Reich, Religiöser und gesellschaftlicher Wandel in Deutschland zwischen 1555 und 1620," *Historische Zeitschrift* 246 (1988): 6, 30; the entire article is found on 1–45 and contains references to the growing bibliography on "confessionalization." See also Schilling's "Reformation und Konfessionalisierung in Deutschland und die neuere deutsche Geschichte," *Gegenwartskunde, Gesellschaft, Staat, Erziehung,* Sonderheft 6 (1988): 11–29, 24.

25. See Bengt Hägglund, "Martin Luther über die Sprache," *Neue Zeitschrift für systematische Theologie und Religionsphilosophie* 26 (1984), 6–11; Paul Althaus, *The Theology of Martin Luther,* trans. Robert C. Schultz (Philadelphia: Fortress, 1966), 35–42; and Gerhard Ebeling, *Luther: An Introduction to His Thought,* trans. R. A. Wilson (Philadelphia: Fortress, 1970), 119–20.

26. "Die Confessio Augustana—Lebendiges Bekenntnis," *Zeitschrift für bayerische Kirchengeschichte* 49 (1980): 136.

27. Martim C. Warth, "The Way to Concord," in *Theologians Convocation: Formula for Concord,* ed. Samuel H. Nafzger (St. Louis: The Lutheran Church—Missouri Synod, 1977), 31–38.

28. Ibid.

29. John M. Headley, "The Reformation as Crisis in the Understanding of Tradition," *Archiv für Reformationsgeschichte* 78 (1987): 7.

30. Ibid., 15.

31. WA 50:570–75; LW 41:81–86.

32. Armin-Ernst Buchrucker, "Die regula atque norma in der Theologie Luthers," *Neue Zeitschrift für systematische Theologie und Religionsphilosophie* 10 (1968): 131–69, esp. 146.

33. Walther von Loewenich, *Wahrheit und Bekenntnis im Glauben Luthers, dargestellt im Anschluss an Luthers Grossen Katechismus* (Wiesbaden: Steiner, 1974), 18, 22.

34. Ibid., 6.

35. Buchrucker, *Neue Zeitschrift für systematische Theologie,* 147.

36. Ibid., 148–50.

37. WA 50:519–26, cf. 543–47; LW 41:20–27, cf. 49–52.

38. What Edmund Schlinck says of confessional documents in this regard is true of all Christian confession, *Theology of the Lutheran Confessions,* trans. Paul F. Koehnecke and Herbert J. A. Bouman (Philadelphia: Muhlenberg, 1961), xvi.

39. See, for example, Martin Greschat, *Melanchthon neben Luther: Studien zur Gestalt der Rechtfertigungslehre zwischen 1528 und 1537* (Witten: Luther, 1965), 59, 90–109.

40. "Revelation and Tradition. Notes on Some Aspects of Doctrinal Continuity in the Theology of Philip Melanchthon," *Studia Theologica* XIII (1959): 97–133.

41. Cochrane, "The Act of Confession-Confessing," 61.

42. Sasse, *Here We Stand,* 4.

43. WA 50:262–83; esp. 262–63, 282; LW 34:201–29, esp. 201–02, 227–28.

44. Cruciger, *Symboli Niceni enarratio, complectens ordine doctrinam Ecclesiae Dei, fideliter recitatem* (Basel, 1550), 10. A portion of this work had been published under the title *De iudiciis piarvm synodorvm Sententia* ... (Wittenberg: Johann Lufft, 1548); cf. Cruciger's *Von den Symbolis und Concilijs: Unterricht* ... (Wittenberg: Georg Rhau, 1548). His friend Joachim Camerarius published *Historia Synodi Nicenae, coactae opera pii studii et religiosae diligentiae Constantini Constantii* ... (Leipzig: Papst, 1552).

45. WA 18:603; LW 33:19–20. According to James D. Tracy in "Two Erasmuses, Two Luthers: Erasmus' Strategy in Defense of *De Libero Arbitrio*," *Archiv für Reformationsgeschichte* 78 (1987): 37–60, Erasmus avoided assertions in part because he held two mutually contradictory views of the freedom of the will. He seemed predisposed to avoid the assuredness of Luther's confessing stance.

46. Gottfried Krodel, "Erasmus—Luther: One Theology, One Method, Two Results," *Concordia Theological Monthly* 41 (1970): 660, 661, 663. Cf. John W. O'Malley, "Erasmus and Luther: Continuity and Discontinuity as Key to their Conflict," *The Sixteenth Century Journal* V, 2 (1974): 47–65; and Wilhelm Maurer, "Offenbarung und Skepsis: Ein Thema aus dem Streit zwischen Luther und Erasmus," in *Wilhelm Maurer, Kirche und Geschichte, Gesammelte Aufsätze, Bd. II, Beiträge zu Grundsatzfragen und zur Frömmigkeitsgeschichte,* ed. Ernst-Wilhelm Kohls and Gerhard Müller (Göttingen: Vandenhoeck & Ruprecht, 1970), 366–402.

47. Ulrich Asendorf, *Luther und Hegel: Untersuchungen zur Grundlegung einer neuen systematischen Theologie* (Wiesbaden: Steiner, 1982), 106.

48. WA 26:261–509; LW 37:161–372, esp. 360.

49. Gottfried Seebass, "Die reformatorischen Bekenntnisse vor der Confessio Augustana," in *Kirche und Bekenntnis,* 26–55. On the development of early Lutheran confessions in the context of negotiations for princely and municipal alliances, see Gerhard Müller, "Bündnis und Bekenntnis: Zum Verhältnis von Glaube und Politik im deutschen Luthertum des 16. Jahrhunderts," in *Bekenntnis und Einheit der Kirche,* 23–43; and also Müller's "Alliance and Confession: The Theological-Historical Development and Ecclesiastical-Political Significance of Reformation Confessions," in *The Formula of Concord: Quadricentennial Essays; The Sixteenth Century Journal* VIII, 4 (1977): 123–40.

50. See Maurer, *Kommentar,* I:18–61, *Historical Commentary,* 3–57; Gottfried Seebass, "'Apologia' und 'Confessio': Ein Beitrag zum Selbstverständnis des Augsburgischen Bekenntnisses," in *Bekenntnis und Einheit der Kirche,* 9–21; Ernst Koch, "Die kursächsischen Vorarbeiten zur Confessio Augustana," in his *Aufbruch und Weg: Studien zur lutherischen Bekenntnisbildung im 16. Jahrhundert* (Berlin: Evangelische Verlagsanstalt, 1983), 7–19.

51. Seebass, *Bekenntnis und Einheit der Kirche,* esp. 15.

52. Rainer Vinke has argued that Luther played almost no role at all in the actual composition of the Augsburg Confession. See "Die Reichstagsgeschehen von Augsburg und die Entstehung der Confessio Augustana unter besonderer Berücksichtigung des Blinkwinkels von der Koburg," paper delivered at the Seventh International Congress for Luther Research, Oslo, Norway, August 1988. Nonetheless, his participation in the formulation of documents which Melanchthon employed as he composed the Augsburg Confession did exert his influence in that process.

53. WA 6:404–69, esp. 412; LW 44:123–217, esp. 135.

54. Elert, "Die Bedeutung der Augsburgischen Konfession im theologischen Denken und in der geistesgeschichtlichen Entwicklung," in *Ein Lehrer der Kirche,* 97–99.

55. *Die Bekenntnisschriften der evangelisch-lutherischen Kirche,* 5th ed. (Göttingen: Vandenhoeck & Ruprecht, 1963), 13–14. *The Book of Concord,* trans. and ed. Theodore G. Tappert et al. (Philadelphia: Fortress, 1959), 13.

56. Bernhard Lohse, "Augsburger Bekenntnis," *Theologische Realenzyklopädie* 4:617.

57. Augsburg Confession, Preface, 8; *Bekenntnisschriften,* 45–46; *The Book of Concord,* 25.

58. In this regard, see Reinhard Schwarz, "Lehrnorm und Lehrkontinuität: Das Selbstverständnis der lutherischen Bekenntnisschriften," in *Bekenntnis und Einheit der Kirche,* 253–70, and Leif Aalen, "Confessio Augustana 1530–1580, Jubiläum oder Mausoleum? Zur Bedeutung des Schrifttheologen Luther für die Augsburgische Konfession und das lutherische Bekenntnis," in *Luther und die Bekenntnisschriften* (Erlangen: Martin Luther Verlag, 1981), 20–45.

59. See n. 54, and Robert C. Schultz, "An Analysis of the Augsburg Confession, Article VII, 2 in Its Historical Context, May & June 1530," *The Sixteenth Century Journal* XI, 3 (1980): 25–35. For a theological analysis, see Hermann Sasse, "Article VII of the Augsburg Confession in the Present Crisis of Lutheranism,"

in *We Confess the Church,* trans. Norman Nagel (St. Louis: Concordia, 1986), 40–68.

60. Augsburg Confession, conclusion to the doctrinal articles; *Bekenntnisschriften,* 83c–83d; *The Book of Concord,* 47. See Ralph A. Bohlmann, *Principles of Biblical Interpretation in the Lutheran Confessions,* 2nd ed. (St. Louis: Concordia, 1983).

61. Augsburg Confession, Preface 3, *Bekenntnisschriften,* 44, *The Book of Concord,* 25.

62. Augsburg Confession, Preface 11, *Bekenntnisschriften,* 46; *The Book of Concord,* 25.

63. Hermann Sasse, "Jesus Christ is Lord: The Church's Original Confession," in *We Confess Jesus Christ,* trans. Norman Nagel (St. Louis: Concordia, 1984), 9–35.

64. *Bekenntnisschriften,* 414, 415, 433; *The Book of Concord,* 291, 292, 302. See Elert, "Der Weg zum kirchlichen Bekenntnis," 95–96.

65. Augsburg Confession, conclusion to the doctrinal articles, 1, *Bekenntnisschriften,* 83c-d, *The Book of Concord,* 47.

66. Sasse, *We Confess Jesus Christ,* 10–11.

67. Georg Heckel, *Zeitschrift für bayerische Kirchengeschichte,* 140.

68. Georg Kretschmar, "Die Bedeutung der Confessio Augustana als verbindliche Bekenntnisschrift der evangelisch-lutherischen Kirche," in Fries et al., *Confessio Augustana,* 62–63.

69. Friedrich-Wilhelm Künneth, "Die bleibende Bedeutung der Konkordienformel," in *Bekenntnis zur Wahrheit,* 164–65.

70. WA Briefe, 5, No. 1568, 319–20.

71. See Martin Heckel, "Die reichsrechtliche Bedeutung der Bekenntnisse," in *Bekenntnis und Einheit der Kirche,* 57–88.

72. See Albrecht Peters, "Zur Aktualität der geistlichen Intention und theologischen Struktur der Confessio Augustana," in *Zur bleibenden Aktualität,* 158–61. On Luther's eschatology, see Robin Bruce Barnes, *Prophecy and Gnosis, Apocalypticism in the Wake of the Lutheran Reformation* (Stanford: Stanford University Press, 1988), esp. 36–53; and Ulrich Asendorf, *Eschatologie bei Luther* (Göttingen: Vandenhoeck & Ruprecht, 1967).

73. Augsburg Confession, Preface, 1–14; *Bekenntnisschriften,* 44–47; *The Book of Concord,* 24–26. Cf. Sasse, *Here We Stand,* 75–84.

74. For a bibliography of the editions of the Augsburg Confession to 1580, see W. H. Neuser, *Bibliographie der Confessio Augustana und Apologie 1530–1580* (Nieuwkoop: De Graaf, 1987).

75. On these efforts at Augsburg, see essays in *Vermittlungsversuche auf dem Augsburger Reichstag 1530, Melanchthon—Brenz—Vehus,* ed. Rolf Decot (Stuttgart: Steiner, 1989). On the efforts surrounding the Wittenberg Concord, see the analysis of James M. Kittelson, "Ecumenism and Condemnation in Luther and Early Lutheranism," *The Lutheran Quarterly,* N. S. 3 (1989): 131–45.

76. Ernst Koch, "Bedeutungswandlungen der Confessio Augustana zwischen 1530 und 1580," in *Aufbruch und Weg,* 20–33.

77. Although the earlier connection between alliance and confession was altered in the period after 1555, as Gerhard Müller observes in "Bündnis und Be-

NOTES

kenntnis," in *Bekenntnis und Einheit der Kirche,* 37–43, and in "Alliance and Confession," in *The Sixteenth Century Journal,* 138–40, the common commitment to the Augsburg Confession—and disagreements over its proper text (see below) certainly did play a significant role in the princely support for efforts toward concord in the 1550s, 1560s, and 1570s. In regard to the legal use of the Confession in the Empire, see Heckel in *Bekenntnis und Einheit der Kirche,* 57–88, 77.

78. Georg Heckel, "Die Confessio Augustana—Lebendiges Bekenntnis," *Zeitschrift für bayerische Kirchengeschichte* 49 (1980): 142–57.

79. For example, see Herbert Immenkötter, "Die Antwort der altgläubigen auf das Augsburger Glaubensbekenntnis der Lutheraner," *Zeitschrift für bayerische Kirchengeschichte* 49 (1980): 123–35, for a partial introduction to the subject. Throughout the 16th century, Roman Catholic polemic focused on the Augsburg Confession.

80. *Bekenntnisschriften,* 84, *The Book of Concord,* 49.

81. Conclusion to the doctrinal articles and introduction to the abuse section of the Augsburg Confession; *Bekenntnisschriften,* 83c–84, *The Book of Concord,* 47–48.80. See also Martin Brecht, "Bekenntnis und Gemeinde" in *Bekenntnis und Einheit der Kirche,* 45–56. On the use of the Confession in specific areas, see Günther Wartenberg, "Die Confessio Augustana in der albertinischen Politik unter Herzog Heinrich von Sachsen," *Zeitschrift für bayerische Kirchengeschichte* 49 (1980): 44–53; Robert Stupperich, "Die Confessio Augustana in Westfalen," *Zeitschrift für westfälische Kirchengeschichte* 75 (1982): 43–56; Gerhard Pfeiffer, "Nürnberg und das Augsburger Bekenntnis 1530–1561," *Zeitschrift für bayerische Kirchengeschichte* 49 (1980): 2–19; and Ludwig Binder, "Die Augsburgische Konfession in der siebenburgischen evangelischen Kirche," *Zeitschrift für bayerische Kirchengeschichte* 49 (1980): 54–85. Wartenberg makes the interesting observation that in the early years "the individual articles of the Confession did not come into consideration for the unfolding of Evangelical teaching and the development of the new ecclesiastical way of life. The Confession was, if at all, appealed to as a whole" (p. 53).

82. Georg Heckel, *Zeitschrift für bayerische Kirchengeschichte,* 49:136.

83. For example, Paul von Eitzen's *Rechte vnd ware meinung vnd verstand Goettlicher Schrifft vnd der Augspurgischen Bekandtnus/Von etlichen Artickelen/ welcher ein schlechte erklerung/itzt noetig ist. Zusamen gezogen aus der Augspurgischen bekandtnus/Die Anno 30. vbergeben ist/Aus der Apologia/Schmalkaldischen Artickeln/vnd Catechismo Lutheri/* ... (Hamburg: Joachim Lewe, 1562).

84. On the medieval understanding of the *sola Scriptura* principle and Biblical authority, see Alister E. McGrath, *The Intellectual Origins of the European Reformation* (Oxford: Basil Blackwell, 1987), esp. 140–74.

85. On these developments, see Robert Kolb, "Die Umgestaltung und theologische Bedeutung des Lutherbildes im späten 16. Jahrhundert," in *Die lutherische Konfessionalisierung in Deutschland. Wissenschaftliches Symposion des Vereins für Reformationsgeschichte 1988,* ed. Hans-Christoph Rublack (Gütersloh: Mohn, 1991).

86. On the development of the ecclesiastical constitutions and the *corpora doctrinae,* see Paul Tschackert, *Die Entstehung der lutherischen und der refor-*

mierten Kirchenlehre samt ihren innerprotestantischen Gegensätzen (Göttingen: Vandenhoeck & Ruprecht, 1910), 572–610; and Gerhard Müller, "Das Konkordienbuch von 1580: Geschichte und Bedeutung," *Zeitschrift für bayerische Kirchengeschichte* 49 (1980): 166–68.

87. WA Briefe, 5, No. 1609, 9f.
88. Ibid., No. 1657, 8f.
89. See Kantzenbach, *Luther-Jahrbuch* 1963, 70–96; Bernhard Lohse, "Glaube und Bekenntnis bei Luther und in der Konkordienformel," in *Widerspruch, Dialog, und Einigung, Studien zur Konkordienformel der lutherischen Reformation,* ed. Wenzel Lohff and Lewis W. Spitz (Stuttgart: Calwer, 1977), 13–40; and Lohse, "Luther und das Augsburger Bekenntnis," in *Das Augsburger Bekenntnis von 1530, Damals und Heute,* ed. Berhard Lohse and Otto Hermann Pesch (Munich: Kaiser, and Mainz: Grünewald, 1980), 144–63.
90. WA Briefe, 5:442.

Chapter 2: The Model Confession

1. WA 3:389.
2. *Georgii Spalatini Annales reformationis Oder Jahr-Buecher von der Reformation Lutheri,* ed. Ernst Solomon Cyprian (Leipzig: Gleditsch and Weidmann, 1718), 134.
3. Mathesius, *Historien Von des Ehwirdigen in Gott Seligen Theuren Manns Gottes, Doctoris Martini Luthers anfang, lehr leben vnd sterben* (Nuremberg, 1566; I have used the edition published there by Berg, 1580), 79r; cf. a similar statement in Nikolaus Selnecker, *Historica Oratio. Vom Leben vnd Wandel des Ehrwirdigen Herrn vnd theuren Mannes Gottes, D. Martini Lutheri* (Wittenberg, 1576), 59v–60r.
4. In the 1578 Latin translation, *Historia Augustanae Confessionis* (Frankfurt/M: Feierabendt, 1578),):(2.
5. Johann Pappus, *Commentarius in confessionem fidei, Anno XXX. in comitiis Augustanis invictiss. imperatori Carolo V. exhibitam, & eiusdem Confessionis Apologiam: publice in Academia Argentoratensi propositus* (Frankfurt/M: Johann Spiess, 1589), +2v.
6. Coelestin, *Historia Comitiorum Anno M.D. XXX. Augustae Celebratorum, repurgatae doctrinae occasionem, praecipuas de religione deliberationes, Consilia, Postulata, Responsa, pacis et concordiae media, Pompas, Epistolas, & tam Pontificiorum quam Euangelicorum scripta pleraque complectens* (Frankfurt/O: Eichorn, 1577), I:A2r; cf. Chytraeus, *Historia Der Augspurgischen Confession* (Rostock: Lucius, 1576), 135v-136r. On this rivalry and the entire subject, see Robert Kolb, "Augsburg 1530: German Lutheran Interpretations of the Diet of Augsburg to 1577," *The Sixteenth Century Journal* XI, 3 (1980): 47–61, especially 57–58 and n. 28; and Rudolf Keller, "David Chytraeus und die Confessio Augustana," in *Die lutherische Konfessionalisierung in Deutschland.* Wissenschaftliches Symposion des Vereins für Reformationsgeschichte 1988, ed. Hans-Christoph Rublack (Gütersloh: Mohn, 1991).
7. Wigand, *Historia de Augustana Confessione* (Königsberg: Daubmann, 1574), 8r.

8. *Confessio augustana versibus elegiacis reddita* (Mühlhausen: Georg Hantzsch, 1575).

9. *Friderici Myconii Historia Reformationis vom Jahr Christi 1517. bis 1542.*, ed. Ernst Solomon Cyprian (Leipzig: Weidmann, 1718), 92.

10. Mathesius, *Historien,* 19r.

11. Wigand, *Historia,* 19r.

12. Mathesius, *Historien,* 76v–77r, 78v–79r.

13. Wigand, *Historia,,* A5.

14. Wigand, *Historia,* 4v, 13v, 6; cf. Wigand's *Tafel oder Richtschnur: jrrige meinung in der Christlichen Kirchen recht zu vrtheilen, Allen Christen bey verlust der Goettlichen warheit noetig zu wissen* (n.p., n.d.), (A)v.

15. Wigand, *Historia,* A2v-A3r.

16. *Confessio Oder Bekentnis des Glaubens/etlicher Fuersten vnd Stedte:Vberantwortet Keiserlicher Maiestat: Zu Augspurg. Anno M.D.XXX. Aus dem eltisten Exemplar/so im 1531. Jar zu Wittenberg ausgangen/von wort zu wort trewlich nachgedruckt,* ed. Johannes Wigand (Königsberg: Georg Osterberg, 1577), Aiij'-(Avj)ʳ.

17. Selnecker, *Oratio,* 50v-51r, 59v-60r.

18. *loci;* note Coelestin's terminology. The Confession itself called them "articles," but in the dogmatic treatises of the Reformation these individual topics were called "commonplaces" [loci communes]. Coelestin and his contemporaries viewed the articles of confessions of faith as the equivalents of the doctrinal loci.

19. Coelestin, *Historia,* I:#4r; II:) (4r; III: (:)3; I:141r, II:190.

20. Chytraeus, *Historia Der Augspurgischen Confession,* 1r, 46, 85v-86r.

21. Wigand, *Historia,* A5v-2r, cf. A2v-A3r, 6r.

22. Selnecker, *Recitationes aliquot. 1. De concilio scripti libri concordiae et modo agendi, qui in subscriptionibus servatus est: 2. De persona Christi et Coena Domini: 3. De autoritate et sententia Confessionis Augustanae: 4. De autoritate Lutheri et Philippi: 5. De controversis nonnullis articulis: . . .* (Leipzig, 1581), 214–16. On the Reformed opposition to this point of view, see Robert Kolb, "Luther, Augsburg, and the Concept of Authority in the Late Reformation, Ursinus vs. the Lutherans," in *Controversy and Conciliation, the Reformation and the Palatinate, 1559–1583,* ed. Derk Visser (Allison Park, PA: Pickwick, 1986), 33–49.

23. Selnecker, *Recitationes,* 163–264.

24. *Die Bekenntnisschriften der evangelisch-lutherischen Kirche,* 5th ed. (Göttingen: Vandenhoeck & Ruprecht, 1963), 3, 9; *The Book of Concord,* translated and edited by Theodore G. Tappert et al. (Philadelphia: Fortress, 1959), 3, 9.

25. Mathesius, *Historien,* 82v-83r.

26. Wigand, *Historia,* 15r.

27. Myconius, *Historia,* 93–94.

28. Spalatin, *Annales,* 132, 138–44, 152–53.

29. Selnecker, *Oratio,* 52v.

30. Ibid., 55v.

31. For the text of the Edict of Worms, see *1521–1971, Luther in Worms,* ed.

Joachim Rogge (Berlin: Evangelische Verlagsanstalt, 1971), 138–55.

32. Hans-Werner Gensichen, *We Condemn: How Luther and 16th-Century Lutheranism Condemned False Doctrine,* trans. Herbert J. A. Bouman (St. Louis: Concordia, 1967).

33. Mathesius, *Historien,* 86r.

34. Chytraeus, 1576 ed., 17v; 1578 Latin ed.,):(2v; Coelestin, *Historia,* II:) (4v.

35. *Bekenntnisschriften,* 46–47; *The Book of Concord,* 26.

36. Helmbold, *Confessio augustana,* [F7]v-[F8]v.

37. Spalatin, *Annales,* 131–32, 189, 198.

38. Mathesius, *Historien,* 76; cf. *Chronicon Carionis* (Frankfurt/M: Braubach, n.d.), 215; Chytraeus, 1576 ed., 89v-90, 188v.

39. Wigand, *Historia,* 10v, 28. Christoph Cörner expressed similar sentiments in his *De confessione fidei et doctrinae Augustae Vindelicorum Carolo V. Rom: Imperatori praelecta & exhibita, Oratio continens ueram & simplicem narrationem errorum, quae sub illud tempus de illa dicta actaque sunt* (Frankfurt/O: Johannes Eichorn, 1568), A3r, Br.

40. Selnecker, *Oratio,* 49v.

41. On these tensions, see Robert Kolb, "Dynamics of Party Conflict in the Saxon Late Reformation, Gnesio-Lutherans vs. Philippists," *The Journal of Modern History* 49 (1977): D1289-1305.

42. Camerarius, *Philippi Melanchthonis ortu, totius vitae curriculo et morte ... Narratio diligens et accurate* (Leipzig: Voegelin, 1566), 124.

43. See Bernhard Lohse, "Augsburger Bekenntnis," *Theologische Realenzyklopädie* 4:625–27.

44. Gallus, *Thema depravationum Augustanae Confessionis et concertationum ... pro servanda veritate eius Confessionis* (Regensburg: Geisler, 1560), esp. B2r; cf. Coelestin, *Historia,* II:229, 231; Wigand, *Historia,* 6v–7.

45. Mathesius, *Historien,* 77v.

46. Selnecker, *Oratio,* 49v, 50v, 52v, 57, 61v–64v. Cörner expressed a similar assessment of the relationship of the two, *De confessione fidei ... Oratio,* Bv-B2r, B5v.

47. Chytraeus, 1578 Latin ed.,):(3r. See Keller, "David Chytraeus."

48. Wigand, *Historia,,* 31v-[50]r.

49. See n. 41 and Robert Kolb, "Historical Background of the Formula of Concord," in *A Contemporary Look at the Formula of Concord,* ed. Robert D. Preus and Wilbert H. Rosin (St. Louis: Concordia, 1978), 12–87, for an overview of the period.

50. E.g., *Confessio Oder Bekentnis des Glaubens/Durch den durchleuchtigsten/ hochgebornen Fursten vnd Herrn Johans Hertzogen zu Sachssen/Churfursten etc.,/vnd etliche Fuersten vnd Stedte/vberantwort Keiserlicher Maiestat/auff dem Reichstag/gehalten zu Augspurg/Anno 1530. . . .* (Wittenberg: Peter Seitz, 1561), containing the 1551 Saxon Confession and the 1555 Visitation Articles of August of Saxony; or *Confessio oder Bekenntnis des Glaubens/etlicher Fursten vnd Stedte/Vberantwort Keiserlicher Maiestat/auff dem Reichstag gehalten zu Augsburgk/Anno 1530* (Wittenberg: Hans Lufft, 1567), with the Apology of the Confession. Extensive alteration appears in Articles 4, on justification; 5, on the

ministry; 13, on the use of the sacraments; 15, on church usages; 20, on faith and good works; 26, on the distinction of foods; and 28, on the power of bishops. In this edition the original wording of Article 10, on the Lord's Supper, is retained. As noted, its alterations caused the initial controversy.

51. On the diet of Naumburg, see Robert Calinich, *Der Naumburger Fürstentag, 1561* (Gotha, 1870).

52. Wigand, *Historia,* 33v–34v; see also the anonymous *Von der Semptlichen Vnter-schreibung der Augspurgischen Confession, darauff jetzundt von etzlichen ge-drungen wirdt* (n.p., 1561), esp. aiiij^r and Bij^v (on the freedom of the will). On the authorship of this tract, see Keller, "David Chytraeus." Nikolaus Gallus (c. 1516–70), a close friend of Wigand, reflected his viewpoint in his *Thema de-pravationvm.* The Gnesio-Lutheran authors of *Confessionschrifft. Etlicher Pre-dicanten in den Herrschafften Graitz, Geraw, Schonburg, vnd anderer hernach vnterschriebenen: Zu Notwendigen Ablenung vieler ertichten Calumnien vnd Lesterungen, vnd dagegen zu erklerung vnd befoerderung der Warheit ...* ([Eisleben, 1567]), E, also set forth a sharply critical examination of the sup-porters of the "altered Augsburg Confession."

53. W. H. Neuser, *Bibliographie der Confessio Augustana und Apologie 1530–1580* (Nieuwkoop: De Graaf, 1987), 15–18.

54. Wigand, *Historia,* 37v–46v. Cf. Wigand's defense of the Augsburg Confession in the brief, popular tract, *Tafel oder Richtschnur.* A brief overview of these de-velopments is given in Gerhard Müller, "Das Konkordienbuch von 1580," *Zeit-schrift für bayerischen Kirchengeschichte* 40 (1980): 163–66. See also Wigand, *Confessio Oder Bekentnis,* [Avij]^r-Bij^r. Cf. the earlier edition of the text, *Die Vnuerfelschete Augspurgische Confession Vnd Schmalcaldische Artickel/Sampt einer Vermanung Joachimi Magdeburgij/an eine Ersame Landschaft Oester-reich* (Regensburg: Geissler, 1561). On Chytraeus' evaluation of the dispute over the text, see Keller, "David Chytraeus."

55. See, e.g., Selnecker's *Recitationes ... ,* esp. 212–63; and the *Apologia, Oder Verantwortung dess Christlichen Concordien buchs ...* (Dresden: Matthes Stoeckel, 1584). On the differing concepts of authority among the Lutherans and the Calvinists, see Kolb, in *Controversy and Conciliation,* and on oppo-sition to the Augsburg Confession in the Reformed camp, *The Sixteenth Century Journal,* 60–61, n. 34. The controversy continued into the next decade; see Aegidius Hunnius, *Articulus siue Locus de sacramentis veteris et noui testa-menti, praecipuis de Baptismo & Coene Domini ...* (Frankfurt/M: Johann Spies, 1590), translated as *Gründtliche vnd aussfuhrliche Beweisung/dass die Zwing-lianer vnnd Caluinisten der der wahren Augspurgischen Confession/Anno 1530. den 25. Junij/Keyser CAROLO V. vbergeben/niemals zugethan gewesen/ vnd sie sich derselbigen noch heutiges tages falschlich beruhmen,* trans. Jeremiah Vietor (Frankfurt/M: Johann Spiess, 1591). On Calvinist reactions toward the Formula of Concord, specifically on Reformed critiques of the Augsburg Confes-sion and the role they played in the Lutheran Church, see the forthcoming study of reactions to the Formula of Concord by Irene Dingel.

Chapter 3: The Situation Demands Confession

1. W. D. Hauschild, "Zum Kampf gegen das Augsburger Interim in norddeutschen Hansestädten," *Zeitschrift für Kirchengeschichte* 84 (1973): 61; cf. Horst Rabe,

Reichsbund und Interim, Die Verfassungs- und Religionspolitik Karls V. und der Reichstag von Augsburg 1547/1548 (Cologne: Böhlau, 1971), esp. on "confessionalization," 92–117.

2. Texts of nine such songs are found in Philip Wackernagel, *Das deutsche Kirchenlied von der ältesten Zeit bis zu Anfang des XVII. Jahrhunderts,* 3 (Leipzig: Teubner, 1870); for those with references to John Frederick's status as confessor, see 1016, 1018–24, 1025–26; others are found on 1009–10, 1012–13, 1024–25, 1027, 1029–30, 1062, 1064.

3. Johann Erdmann Bieck, *Das Dreyfache Interim* (Leipzig, 1721), 31.

4. *Formula reformationis per Caesaream Maiestatem Statibus Ecclesiasticis in Comitijs Augustanis ad deliberandum proposita, et ab eisdem vt paci publice consulerent, & per eam Ecclesiarum ac Cleri sui vtilitati commodius prouiderent, probata & recepta* (Augsburg, 1548). Joachim Mehlhausen has edited the text of the Interim, *Das Augsburger Interim von 1548, Deutsch und lateinisch* (Neukirchen: Neukirchener Verlag, 1970).

5. On this debate, see Franz Lau and Ernst Bizer, *A History of the Reformation in Germany to 1555,* trans. Brian A. Hardy (London: Black, 1969), 210-11, who agree with Leopold von Ranke, that Charles originally intended the Interim to regulate church life throughout the empire; Gustav Wolf, "Das Augsburger Interim," *Deutsche Zeitschrift für Geschichtswissenschaft* NF II (1897–98): 84–87, agrees. Others argue that Charles always intended to enforce the Interim only in Evangelical lands; see, e.g., Georg Beutel, *Über den Ursprung des Augsburger Interims* (Dresden: Paessler, 1888), 107–16, and Walther von Loewenich, "Das Interim von 1548," in *Von Augustin zu Luther* (Witten: Luther, 1959), 394. On the resulting controversies over the Augsburg Interim and the Saxon compromise, the Leipzig Interim, see Joachim Mehlhausen, "Der Streit um die Adiaphora," in *Bekenntnis und Einheit der Kirche, Studien zum Konkordienbuch,* ed. Martin Brecht and Reinhard Schwarz (Stuttgart: Calwer, 1980), 105–28; Jobst Schöne, "Von den Grenzen kirchlicher Freiheit, Die Aussage des Artikel X der Konkordienformel über die Adiaphora," in *Bekenntnis zur Wahrheit, Aufsätze über die Konkordienformel,* ed. Jobst Schöne (Erlangen: Martin Luther, 1978), 113–20; Oliver K. Olson, "Politics, Liturgics, and *Integritas Sacramenti,*" in *Discord, Dialogue, and Concord: Studies in the Lutheran Reformation's Formula of Concord,* ed. Lewis W. Spitz and Wenzel Lohff (Philadelphia: Fortress, 1977), 74–85.

6. Hans Christoph von Hase, *Die Gestalt der Kirche Luthers, Der casus confessionis im Kampf des Matthias Flacius gegen das Interim von 1548* (Göttingen: Vandenhoeck & Ruprecht, 1940), 17.

7. On how this process worked, see Thomas A. Brady, Jr., *Ruling Class, Regime and Reformation at Strasbourg, 1520–1555* (Leiden: Brill, 1978), 259–90; and Gerhard Pfeiffer, "Die Stellungnahme der Nürnberger Theologen zur Einführung des Interims 1548," in *Humanitas-Christianitas, Walther v. Loewenich zum 65. Geburtstag,* ed. Karlmann Beyschlag, Gottfried Maron, and Eberhard Wolfel (Witten: Luther Verlag, 1968), 111–33.

8. Philip Melanchthon, *Opera quae supersunt omnia, Corpus reformatorum* (Halle: Schwetschke, 1834–60), VI:925.

9. *Bedencken auffs Interim Des Ehrwirdigen vnd Hochgelarten Herrn Philippi Melanthonis* (n.p., 1548), Aijʳ-Aiijʳ.

10. See Mehlhausen, "Streit," 111–15; von Hase, *Gestalt der Kirche,* 16.

11. Ibid., 48–53; Mehlhausen, "Streit," 105–7.

12. The text of the Leipzig Interim and the series of memoranda leading to it are found in *Corpus reformatorum,* VI:839–45, 853–57, 865–74, 888–90, 908–12, 924–42, VII: 12–45. On these developments, see Luther D. Peterson, "The Philippist Theologians and the Interims of 1548: Soteriological, Ecclesiastical, and Liturgical Compromises and Controversies within German Lutheranism," Ph.D. dissertation, The University of Wisconsin, 1974.

13. Lau and Bizer, *Reformation,* 213–15.

14. This analysis of the parties is given in detail in Robert Kolb, "Dynamics of Party Conflict in the Saxon Late Reformation: Gnesio-Lutherans vs. Philippists," *The Journal of Modern History* 49 (1977):D1289–1305.

15. *Antwort, Glaub vnd Bekentnis auff das schoene vnd liebliche INTERIM* (Magdeburg: Lotther, 1548), Aij; cf. *Der Prediger der Jungen Herrn Johans Friederichen Hertzogen zu Sachssen etc. Soenen Christlich Bedencken auff das INTERIM* (n.p., 1548). On the eschatological thrust in Lutheran theology in this period, see Robin Bruce Barnes, *Prophecy and Gnosis: Apocalypticism in the Wake of the Lutheran Reformation* (Stanford, CA: Stanford University Press, 1988), esp. 64–65.

16. *Das Doctor Martinus kein Adiaphorist gewesen ist vnd Das D. Pfeffinger vnd das buch on namen jhm gewalt vnd vnrecht thut* (Magdeburg: Roedinger, 1550), Aiij^v-Bij^v.

17. *Bekentnuss vnd Erklerung auffs Interim. Durch der Erbarn Stedte, Luebeck, Hamburg, Lueneburg etc . . .* (Magdeburg: Lotter, 1548). See Hauschild, *Zeitschrift für Kirchengeschichte* 84:60–81.

18. Ibid., 84:60.

19. *Homiliae qvatvor de custodiendo precioso thesauro verbi Dei & cultus sacri, contra multiplices fures, Papistas, Interimistas & Adiaphoristas, deque afflicta Ecclesia Christi non deserenda* (Magdeburg: Lotther, 1550), (A6)v. Westphal issued these sermons in German as well, *Vier Predigten, das man den tewren schatz Goettlichs worts, vnnd des rechten Gottesdiensts bewaren sol, wider die vielfeltigen Diebe, die Papisten, Interimisten vnd Adiaphoristen* (n.p., 1550). He had enunciated these principles the previous year in *Explicatio generalis sententiae, Quod e duobus malis minussit eligendum, ex qua facile quiuis intelligere potest, quid in praesenti de adiaphoris controversia sequendum aut fugiendum sit* (n.p., 1549). See Hauschild, *Zeitschrift für Kirchengeschichte.*

20. *Homiliae,* B2v, B5.

21. *Verlegung des Gruendlichen Berichts der Adiaphoristen, zu diesen boesen zeiten, sehr nuetzlich zu lesen* (n.p., 1551), (Giiij)v-Hr.

22. Hermann, *Das man in diesen geschwinden leufften, dem Teuffel vnd Antichrist zugefallen, nichts in der Kirchen Gottes vorendern soll* (n.p., 1548); Waremund, *Eine gemeine protestation vnd Klagschrifft aller frommen Christen wieder das Interim vnnd andere geschwinde anschlege vnd grausame verfolgung der wiedersacher des Evangelij, allen Gotfuerchtigen gewissen, zu dieser betruebten zeit . . .* (n.p., 1548); Henetus, *Ein kurtzer Bericht vom Interim, daraus man leichtlich kan die leer vnd Geist desselbigen Buchs erkennen* (n.p., 1548); Lauterwar, *Wider das Interim. Papistische Mess, Canonem, vnnd Meister Eissleuben* (n.p., 1549).

23. See von Hase, *Gestalt der Kirche*, 36–37.

24. *Wider den Euangelisten des heiligen Chorrocks, D. Geitz Maior* ("Basel" [Magdeburg], 1552).

25. *Eine schrift M. Flacij Illyrici widder ein recht epicurisch buch, darine das Leiptzische INTERIM verteidiget wird, sich zuhueten fuer den verfelschern der waren Religion* (n.p., 1549), (Aiiij)v.

26. Gallus, *Gegenbericht auff D. Pfeffingers vnd der Adiaphoristen gesuchte glosen vber jhr Leiptzigsch Interim, mit einer trewen warnung an alle Christen* (Magdeburg: Lotther, 1550), Biiijʳ.

27. An incomplete bibliography of the publications issued from Magdeburg in these years is found in Friedrich Hülsse, "Beiträge zur Geschichte der Buchdruckerkunst in Magdeburg," *Geschichts-Blätter für Stadt und Land Magdeburg*, XVII (1882): 150–81, 211–42, 358–97.

28. *Das alle verfolger der Kirchen Christi zu Magdeburgk, Christi des Herrn selbs verfolget sindt. Geschrieben zur warnung an alle Christen, vnd sonderlich an das Kriegsvolck des Feindes* (Magdeburg: Lotther, 1551), Bʳ; see Barnes, 76–77, 105–06 on other eschatological expressions in Flacius.

29. Mehlhausen, "Streit," 125; cf. Hauschild, *Zeitschrift für Kirchengeschichte*, 63.

30. Koch, "Der Weg zur Konkordienformel," in *Vom Dissensus zum Konsensus, Die Formula Concordiae von 1577* (Hamburg: Lutherisches Verlagshaus, 1980), 13.

31. von Hase, *Gestalt der Kirche*, 52–56.

32. Flacius, *Ein Buch, von waren vnd falschen Mitteldingen . . .* (Magdeburg, 1549), Alʳ, in Latin, *Liber de veris et falsis Adiaphoris, quo integre propemodum Adiaphorica controuersia explicatur* (Magdeburg, 1549). Von Hase, *Gestalt der Kirche*, 53–59, provides a detailed summary of Flacius's argument, with copious quotations. Not only Flacius but also Gallus continued to argue this position; see Gallus's tracts from a decade later, *Das die gruende Nicolai Galli noch fest stehen, wider den Adiaphoristen Acta vnd Auszug . . .* (Regensburg: Geissler, 1560), and *Abfertigung, Der vngenenten Wittembergischen Lester Scribenten. Vnd manung Der Professoren selb, zu gebuerlicher rechtschaffner Disputation, vnd ausfuerung jhrer eigen sachen* (Regensburg: Geisler, 1561), both in reply to attacks from the electoral Saxon theologians.

33. Flacius, *Buch, von waren vnd falschen Mitteldingen*, Alᵛ.

34. Ibid., Q3

35. *Responsio M. Nic. Galli et M. Fla. Illyr: ad quarundam Misnensium Concionatorum literas, de quaestione, An potius cedere, quam lineam uestem induere debeant* (Magdeburg, Rhodius, n.d. [ca. 1551]), A5r.

36. Flacius, *Gruendliche verlegung aller Sophisterei, so Juncker Isleb, D. Interim . . . gebrauchen* (n.p., 1550), H2v.

37. Von Hase, *Gestalt der Kirche*, 67.

38. Ibid., 67–71.

39. *Bekentnis Vnterricht vnd vermanung der Pfarbern vnd Prediger der Christlichen Kirchen zu Magdeburgh* (Magdeburg: Lotther, 1550). See Oliver K. Olson, "Theology of Revolution: Magdeburg, 1550–1551," *The Sixteenth Century Journal* III, 1 (1972): 56–79.

40. E.g., in the works of Matthaeus Judex; see Robert Kolb, "Matthaeus Judex's

Condemnation of Princely Censorship of Theologians' Publications," *Church History* 50 (1981): 401–14.

41. Von Hase discusses Flacius's treatment of the roles of church and state, *Gestalt der Kirche,* 71–96.

42. Flacius, *Contra quaedam interimistica & Adiaphoristica scripta, quae a multis Gasparo Huberino tribuuntur . . . Item locus Brentij, praesentibus Christi & Belial Conciliationibus admodum conueniens* (Magdeburg: Rhodius, n.d.). Brenz elaborated on his ideas cited here in his *Evangelion quod inscribitur Secundum Ioannem, Centum Quinquagintaquatuor Homilijs explicatum* (Frankfurt/M: Brubach, 1554), 655. The theme of confessing the faith is treated in others of Brenz's commentaries at appropriate places also; see, e.g., *In evangelii quod inscribitur secundum Lucam, duodecim priora Capita Homiliae Centum & Decem* (Schwäbisch Hall: Brubach, 1538), 308r–09r, where Brenz associated confessing the faith with persecution in commenting on Luke 12:8.

43. Rabus, *Tomvs I. de S. Dei confessoribvs, veteris. qve ecclesiae martyribus . . .* (Strassburg: Heirs of Balthasar Beck, 1552); and *Der Heyligen ausserwoehlten Gottes Zeugen, Bekennern vnd Martyrern . . . Historien* (Strassburg: Heirs of Balthasar Beck, 1552; subsequent vols. II-VIII, Strassburg: Emmel, 1554–58). On Rabus's martyrology, see Robert Kolb, *For All the Saints: Changing Perceptions of Martyrdom and Sainthood in the Lutheran Reformation* (Macon, GA: Mercer University Press, 1987), chapter II.

44. *Der Heyligen . . . Historien,* III:iij-Cijʳ; cf. Johannes Wigand, *Methodus doctrinae Christi sicut in ecclesia Magdeburgensi traditur* (Frankfurt/M: Brubach, 1564), 2–4.

45. *Tomvs I.,* iij-) (ij.

46. *Der Heyligen . . . Historien,* II:ij.

47. Ibid., III:ij.

48. Rabus, *Der Heyligen . . . Historien,* IV:ij-)(r. Rabus expressed similar sentiments in his second edition, *Historien der Martyrer . . .* (Strassburg: Josias Rihel, 1571/1572), II:Aij-Aiiij.

49. *Der Heyligen . . . Historien,* VIII:ijʳ.

50. Ibid., VII:ij-)(iijʳ.

51. Ibid., II:ijʳ-)(.

52. On Luther's concept of the joyous exchange, see Friedrich Wilhelm Kantzenbach, "Christusgemeinschaft und Rechtfertigung. Luthers Gedanke vom fröhlichen Wechsel als Frage an unsere Rechtfertigungsbotschaft," *Luther* 35 (1964): 34–45, and Erwin Iserloh, "Luther und die Mystik," *The Church, Mysticism, Sanctification, and the Natural in Luther's Thought,* ed. Ivar Asheim (Philadelphia: Fortress, 1967), 71–75. On Luther's theology of the cross, see Walther von Loewenich, *Luther's Theology of the Cross,* trans. Herbert J. A. Bouman (Minneapolis: Augsburg, 1976).

53. *Der Heyligen . . . Historien,* II:)(.

54. Ibid., VI:ij-*iiijʳ.

55. *Historien der Martyrer,* I:aij-aiij.

56. *Der Heyligen . . . Historien,* III:ij.

57. Ibid., V:iijʳ-)(.

58. Ibid., VI:ij-*iiij^r.

59. Ibid., I:iij^r.

60. Ibid., IV:)(^{r},)(ij^r; V:)(iij^v-)(iiij; VI:*ij^v-iiij.

61. Ibid., VIII:ij-(vj).

62. See, e.g., Matthias Flacius, *Vermanung zur gedult vnd glauben zu Gott, in Creutz diser verfolgung/geschrieben an die Kirche Christi zu Magdeburg* (Magdeburg: Roedinger, 1551); Joachim Magdeburg, pastor in Hamburg, *Eyne schoene Artzney, dadurch der Leiden den Christen Sorge vnd Trubmus gelindert/Vnd der vngedult im Creutz kan fuergekomen vnd gewereth werden* ... (Lübeck: Richolffen, 1555; preface dated April 1, 1553); Cyriakus Spangenberg, *Epistolae Aliquot consolatoriae, piae et utiles, maxime ijs qui propter confessionem ueritatis persecutiones patiunter* (Strassburg: Samuel Emmel, 1565). This volume contains letters relating to the persecution and exile of Simon Haliaeus, a Bohemian Evangelical pastor, published with an appeal to Emperor Maximilian II. That preface does not address the subject of confession or martyrdom but rather appeals for support for the Evangelical cause from the emperor, who was widely thought to have been holding secret Protestant sympathies. This suggests that Spangenberg believed that the bold confession and willingness to suffer martrydom which Evangelicals like Haliaeus displayed would commend their faith to the emperor.

63. Wigand, *De persecutione piorvm. Exiliis piorvm. Exiliis facinorsorvm. Martyriis piorvm. Pseudomartyriis. Fvga ministrorvm verbi. Constantia. Apostasia. Patientia.* (Franfkurt/M: Corvinus, 1580), 9-61, cf. 147–73. Echoes of Wigand's treatment are heard in the homiletical treatment of persecution and martyrdom found in the postil of his close friend and associate (also exiled from Jena and Magdeburg) Matthaeus Judex, *Epistolarum festivalium, quae in praecipuis sanctorum feriis, ... proponi solent, Explicatio* (Eisleben: Andreas Petri, 1578), 25v-28r, on the epistle for the festival of Saint Stephen.

64. Wigand, *De persecutione,* 62–74.

65. Ibid., 77–80, 173–74, 282–368.

66. Ibid., 81–146, 215–81.

67. *Recitationes aliquot ... De authoritate et sententia Confessionis Augustanae* ... (Leipzig, 1581), 212–68.

68. See Johannes Brenz's letter to Amsdorf, February 29, 1546, *Corpus reformatorum* VI:65–66.

69. von Hase, *Gestalt der Kirche,* 73.

Chapter 4: Confessing in Controversy

1. I am indebted to Dr. Ernst Koch of the Theologisches Seminar in Leipzig, Germany, for his help in learning more of this controversy. On it, see Georg Buchwald on Poach in *Allgemeine Deutsche Biographie* (Berlin: Humblot, 1888) 27: 325–31; Reinhold Jauernig, *Luther in Thüringen* (Berlin: Evangelische Verlagsanstalt, 1953), 199–200, Erich Kleineidam, *Universitas Studii Erfordensis,* Bd. 3 (Leizpig: St. Benno, 1983), 99–100, and Joachim Meisner, *Nachreformatorische Katholische Frömmigkeitsformen in Erfurt* (Leipzig: St. Benno, 1971), 234–38.

2. This report is printed in the report of the city council, *Gruendlicher vnnd*

warhafftiger Bericht/vnser des Raths zu Erffurdt/aus was bestendigen vrsachen/ die beide Pfarrer zun Barfussern vnd zu Sanct Thomas/Auch jrs beide anhangende Capellan/von jrem Dienst vnd Ampt/enturloubt worden (Erfurt: Melchior Sachsen, 1572), Biijʳ–Cʳ.

3. *Eine Predigt/darinnen angezeiget/vnd aus Gottes heiligen warem Wort beweiset wird/wie fehrliche vnd schrecklich es sey/mit den Gottlosen/halsstarrigen/vnbusfertigen Suendern/welche bleiben im vnglauben/vnd ploetzlich vberfallen werden.* (Erfurt, 1571), and *Die letzte Predigt/M. Georgij Silberschlags/gethan aus dem ersten Buch Mosi am 35. Capittel/Anno 1572. am Sontage Sexigesimae da er des Sonnabendts hernach verschieden ist* (Mühlhausen: Georg Hantzsch, 1572).

4. *Eine Predigt aus dem Propheten Hosea, Cap: 4. Vber der Leiche M. Georgij Silberschlags . . . ,* published together with another sermon that dealt with issues regarding the controversy, *Ein ander Predigt, Vber den Spruch Elieae I. Reg: 18. . . .* (n.p., 1572).

5. *Grundlicher vnd warhafftiger Bericht,* Aijʳ–Aiijʳ.

6. Hesshus, *Vom Bekentnis des Namens Jhesu Christi/fuer den Menschen* (originally Jena, 1571; I have used the Erfurt: Conrad Heinrich Preuser, 1587 ed.), with the republished section appearing on [Nvij]ʳ–[Oviij]ʳ: *Frage. Ob ein rechtgleubiger Christ, mit Vnchristen als mit Juden, Tuercken, Heiden oder mit offentlichen vberfuerten Ketzern, Lesterern, vnd Goetzendienern, als mit Sacramentsfeinden, Papisten, Wider teuffern, Moenche vnd Pfaffen, oder auch mit offentlichem Epicurern vnd Suendern, die im bewusten Ehebruch vnd andern lasten ligen, muege Buergerliche gemeinschafft haben, mit jnen essen vnd trincken etc. Antwort Doct: Tilemani Heshusii* (Jena, 1572), Aijʳ–Aiijʳ.

7. Ibid., Aiijʳ–Biiijʳ.

8. *De confessione in doctrina diuina & necessarijs factis* (Jena: Christian Rhode, 1569), A2ʳ.

9. See Hans Werner Gensichen, *We Condemn: How Luther and 16th-Century Lutheranism Condemned False Doctrine,* trans. Herbert J. A. Bouman (St. Louis: Concordia, 1967).

10. On Andreae's first attempts at concord in this period, see Robert Kolb, *Andreae and the Formula of Concord: Six Sermons on the Way to Lutheran Unity* (St. Louis: Concordia, 1977).

11. *De nevtralibvs et mediis pia et necessaria admonitio* (Frankfurt/M: Peter Brubach, 1552), 3, 142.

12. Hesshus, *Vom Bekentnis des Namens Jhesu,* Cijʳ–ᵛ; on the Libertines and the Family of Love, see George Hunston Williams, *The Radical Reformation* (Philadelphia: Westminister, 1962), 351–55, 477–82.

13. Hesshus, *Vom Bekentnis des Names Jhesu,* Ciijʳ–Ciiijʳ; cf. Fvʳ, Jiijʳ.

14. *De confessione,* A2ʳ–A5ʳ, [B6]ʳ; Hᵛ–H3ᵛ.

15. Ibid., [A6]ʳ–[A7]ᵛ.

16. *Explicatio Epistolae Pavli ad Romanos* (Jena: Huttich, 1572), 340v–341r. Cf. similar comments by Wigand, in *In epistolam S. Pauli ad Romanos annotationes* (Frankfurt/M: Corvinus, 1580), 116r, 117v.

17. *Die erste vnd ander Epistel des heyligen Apostels S. Pauli an die Thessalonicher . . .* (Strassburg: Emmel, 1564), xxiiijʳ–xxvᵛ; *Ausslegung der Letsten Acht Capitel*

der Episteln S. Pavli an die Roemer (Strassburg, 1569), ciij^r–cviij^r.

18. *Vermanung zu warer Gottseliger/Christlicher vnd bestendiger Bekendtnis/mit allen jren eigenschafften/darauff sei gegruendet vnd erbawet sein sol* (Eisleben: Urban Gaubisch, 1562), Fij^r.

19. *De confessione*, [A8]^r–B2^r.

20. *Etliche Hohe vnd wichtige Vrsachen/ warumb ein iglicher Christ/ wes Standes er auch ist/ schuldig vnnd pflichtig sey zu jeder zeit/ Sonderlich aber jtzt/ seines glaubens vnd Lere offentliche Bekentnis zu thun/ muendlich/ vnd da ers vermag auch Schrifftlich* (Regensburg: Geisler, 1560), aij^r–biiij [aiiij]^r.

21. *Confession oder Bekentnis Gotlicher reiner/heilsamer Lere von den fuernemesten Artickeln des Glaubens/sampt etlicher widerwertigen Lere/Corruptelen vnd Irthum/kurtze vnd gegruente widerlegung* (Erfurt: Isaiah Mechler, 1582), A5^r–^{v}.

22. *De confessione*, B3^r–[B6]^r; [G8]^r–H^v, [H8]^r–^{v}.

23. Hesshus, *Vom Bekentnis des Namens Jhesu*, Aiij^r, [Bviij]^r–C^r, Cv^v–[Cvj]^r, E^r–[Fvij]^r. The example of Spiera was frequently used as an outstanding example of apostasy, see Robert Kolb, *For All the Saints, Changing Perceptions of Martyrdom and Sainthood in the Lutheran Reformation* (Macon, GA: Mercer University Press, 1987), 63.

24. *Etliche Hohe vnd wichtige Vrsachen*, [cvij]^{r}–d^v.

25. *Gruendtliche vnd richtige Antwort auff die Frage: Ob eine gantze Christliche Gemein/vnd ein jeder Christ insonderheit/von Gottes wegen recht vnd macht habe/allerley Lere zu vrtheilen vnd zu richten/dawider jetziger zeit abermal von etlichen Klueglingen gestrieten vnd gehandelt wird* (Eisleben: Andreas Petri, 1570), esp. 5r–48r.

26. *Christlich bedencken/Ob vnd wie fern ein jglicher Christ/die Rotten vnd Secten/ auch allerley offentliche Irthumen vnd Religionstreitte/beide von Rechts wegen/vnd auch mit der that/zu richten vnd zu anathamatiziren/schuldig sey. Wider etlicher Epicurischen Theologen vnd Clamanten furgeben/als solten die Leien nicht schuldig sein/offentliche Ketzereien zu verdammen. Vnd zur noetigen vermanung an alle Christen/auch jtzt alle schwebende Secten vnd Corrupteln zu richten/vnd wider dieselbigen zu streitten* (n.p., 1562).

27. Scheitlich, *Vermanung zu warer . . . Bekendtnis*, Aiij^r–^{v}.

28. *De confessione*, B4^r.

29. *Vom Bekentnis des Namens Jhesu*, Aij^r, Fiiij^r–^{v}, Kij^r–Kiiij^v.

30. *Etliche Hohe vnd wichtige Vrsachen*, Av^v–Bij^v.

31. *De confessione*, C5^v–[C6]^r.

32. Ibid., [C6]^r–]C7]^r; cf. Hesshus, *Vom Bekentnis des Namens Jhesu*, Gv^v–Hij^r.

33. Wigand, *De confessione*, [C7]^r; Hesshus, *Vom Bekentnis des Namens Jhesu*, Gij^v–Giij^r.

34. Wigand, *De confessione*, [C7]^v–D3^v.

35. Ibid., E4^r–[E7]^r.

36. Spangenberg, *Etliche Hohe vnd wichtige Vrsachen*, ev^r–[evj]^r.

37. Ibid., [dvj].

38. Hesshus, *Vom Bekentnis des Namens Jhesu*, L^v–Liiij^v; cf. WA 30, III:558–71.

39. Hesshus, *Vom Bekentnis des Namens Jhesu*, Lv^v–Miij^v. Both the sons of John

Frederick the Elder married daughters of the Calvinist Elector Frederick III of the Palatinate. Hesshus had served both these princes and may well have been relating an incident at the time of the marriage of one or the other of them.

40. Ibid., Miij^r–Mv^v. On Luther's changing attitude on the necessity of receiving both the body and the blood, see Hermann Sasse, *This is my body, Luther's Contention for the Real Presence in the Sacrament of the Altar* (Minneapolis: Augsburg, 1959), 89–99.

41. Hesshus, *Vom Bekentnis des Namens Jhesu,* [Mvj]^r–[Nvij]^r.

42. Ibid., [Nvij]^r–[Oviij]^r.

43. *Confessio Das ist: Bekendtnuss Caspar Angelanders/des Blinden Pfarrers/ in seinem langwirigen Creutz vnd Elendt/des alters 63. Jhar. Auss heiliger Goettlicher Schrifft/vnd Buechern des Ehrwirdigen in Gott seligen Herren Doctor Martini Luthers, Philippi, Brentij, & c. zusamen gezogen/mit etlichen kurtzen Artickeln Lutheri/Lateinisch vnd Deutsch/Allen frommen/Christlicher Haussvetern/vnd gemeinen Mann nuetzlich zu lesen* (Erfurt: Georg Bawman, 1589).

44. Particularly members of the Gnesio-Lutheran party seemed most inclined to issue personal confessions, e.g. Tileman Hesshus, *Confessio de praesentia corporis et sanguinis Iesu Christi in coene Domini* (Königsberg: Daubmann, 1574), and *Bekandtnus von der Formula Concordiae . . .* (Regensburg: Burger, 1578). In the course of the inner tensions within the Gnesio-Lutheran movement over the doctrine of original sin, several participants issued personal confessions, e.g., that of Christoph Irenaeus, Martin Wolff, Matthias Schneider, and Jonas Franck, *Bekentniss von diesen zweyen Propositionen oder reden, Peccatum Originis est Substantia Vnd Peccatum Originis est Accidens . . .* (Eisleben: Petri? 1572), prepared for presentation before the ducal Saxon consistory in Jena for a hearing on January 3, 1572; and Hieronymus Peristerius, *Christliche Confession vnd Bekentnus/ auch Antwort vnd Bericht . . . von dem gegenwertigen Streite/ der Erbsuende* (n.p., 1574), prepared in reply to a summons from the Regensburg city council. Matthias Flacius reproduced the confession of Alcuin for publication as a means of attacking contemporaries from the "radical" camp, *Albini seu Alcuini Caroli Magni praeceptoris confessio aut doctrina de Deo, compendio exposita, & nunquam antea impressa. Confessio M. Flac. Illyrici de sancrosancta Trinitate contra Seruetianos, Stencfeldianos, & alios seductores ac mendaces* (n.p., 1557). The Philippist opponents of the Gnesio-Lutherans seldom issued personal confessions, but one of their number, Nikolaus Selnecker, did so in an effort to establish his own orthodoxy on issues under dispute at the time for those who might judge him outside electoral Saxony, *Kurtze/ Wahre vnd Einfeltige Bekantnus D. Nic. Selnecceri/ Von der Maiestet, Auffarth/ Sitzen zur Rechten Gottes/ vnd vom Abendmal vnsers HERRN Jhesu Christi . . .* (Heinrichstadt, 1571). A decade later Selnecker republished the confession of the pioneering lay reformer of Nuremberg, the city secretary Lazarus Spengler, *Herrn Lazari Spenglers . . . ware/vnd in Gottes Wort gegrundte Bekentnis/der Artickel vnsers Christlichen Glaubens . . . Mit einer kurtzer Praefation D. Nicolai Selnecceri/ sampt angehefften wenigen Artickeln von der Person Christi/vnd vom Heiligen Abendmal/damit er sich also erkleret/das er durch Gottes gnad schlects bey solcher Bekentnis biss zum Richterstuel Jesu Christi bleiben wolle . . .* (Leipzig: Jacob Baerwaldt's heirs, 1582).

45. The Gnesio-Lutheran theological faculty at the University of Jena also issued position papers under the title "confession": *Bekentnis. von der Rechtfertigung fur Gott. vnd Von guten Wercken.* (Jena: Roedinger, 1569); *Bekentnis Vom Freien Willen. So im Colloquio zu Altenburg, hat sollen voerbracht werden, von Fuerstlichen Sechsischen Theologen* (Jena, 1570); *Bekentnis Vom Fuenff Streittigen Religions Artickeln* (Jena: Roedinger, 1569).

46. The Hamburg ministerium issued its *Der Prediger tho Hamborch Slichte unde Rechte Bekentenisse/von dem Hochwirdigen Sacramente/des Lyues vnd Blodes unsers leuen Heren Jesu Christi . . .* (Hamburg: Johan Wickradt the younger, 1557); the ministerium in Bremen issued both its own statement and a personal statement of Hesshus regarding his recent defense of the Lutheran doctrine of the Lord's Supper in the Palatinate, *Der Prediger zu Bremen Bekantniss/vom Nachtmal Jesu Christi. Vnd Doctoris Tilemani Heshusij Bekantniss vom Nachtmal Jesu Christi. Dem Churfursten Pfaltzgrauen beym Rein vberantwortet . . .* (Magdeburg: Wolffgang Kirchener, 1561). At the beginning of the "crypto-Calvinist" dispute in northern Germany, critiques of the position of the electoral Saxon theologians and their efforts to introduce their views as public teaching took the title "confession," e.g. *Wiederholte Christliche Gemeine Confession vnd Erklerung: Wie in den Sechsischen Kirchen vermoege der heiligen Schrifft/ vnd Augspurgischen Confession/nach der alten Grundtfest D. Lutheri/wieder die Sacramentirer gelehrt wirdt: Vom Abendmal des HERRN. Von der Personlichen vereinigung der Gottlichen vnd Menschlichen Natur in Christo. von seiner Himelfarth/Vnd Sitzen zur Rechten Gottes. . . .* (Heinrichstadt: Cunrad Horn, 1571). The electoral Saxon theologians defended their position in *Kurtz Bekentnis vnd Articel vom heiligen Abendmal des Leibs vnd Bluts Christi. Daraus klar zu sehen/was hievon in beiden Vniuersiteten/Leipzig vnd Wittenberg/vnd sonst in allen Kirchen vnd Schulen des Churfursten zu Sachssen/bisher offentlich geleret/gegleubt vnd bekant worden . . . Vbergeben vnd gehandelt in jungstem Landtag zu Torgau* (Wittenberg: Hans Lufft, 1574), issued also in Latin translation as *Confessio paucis articulis complectens summam doctrinae de vera praesentia Corporis & Sanguinis Christi in Coena dominica . . .* (Wittenberg: Hans Lufft, 1574).

47. For the most part this study does not analyze the confessions written in this period by Lutherans in Scandinavia and in eastern Europe. Texts of a variety of confessions from eastern Europe are edited in *Confessiones ecclesiarum Evangelico-Reformatarum A.C. et H.C. Europae Centro-Orientalis tempore Reformationis III/1, 1546–1576, Ostmitteleuropas Bekenntnisschriften der Evangelischen Kirche A. und H.B. des Reformationszeitalters III/1, 1546–1576,* ed. Peter F. Barton and László Makkai (Budapest, 1987). See also see David P. Daniel, "The Acceptance of the Formula of Concord in Slovakia," *Archiv für Reformationsgeschichte* 70 (1979): 261–63; and Ernst Binder, "Die Augsburgische Konfession in der siebenburgischen evangelischen Kirche," *Zeitschrift für bayerische Kirchengeschichte* 49 (1980): 54–85.

48. See Robert Kolb, "The Advance of Dialectic in Lutheran Theology: The Role of Johannes Wigand (1523–1587)," in *Regnum, Religio et Ratio: Essays Presented to Robert M. Kingdon,* ed. Jerome Friedman (Kirksville, MO: Sixteenth Century Journal Publishers, 1987), 93–102.

49. *Repetitio Confessionis Augustanae, sive Confessio Doctrinae Saxonicarum Ecclesiarum,* in Philip Melanchthon, *Opera Quae supersunt omnia, Corpus*

Reformatorum (Halle: Schwetschke, 1834–60), XXVIII:369–77 (Latin), 481–589 (German).

50. *Confessio Virtembergica, Das württembergische Bekenntnis von 1551,* ed. Ernst Bizer (7. Sonderheft der *Blatter für Württembergische Kirchengeschichte,* Stuttgart: Quell, 1952), 137–38, 188–90. On Brenz's view of church and state, see James Martin Estes, *Christian Magistrate and State Church: The Reforming Career of Johannes Brenz* (Toronto: University of Toronto Press, 1982), esp. 35–58.

51. Specific occasions for the composition of confessions did arise apart from the conflicts in which the Gnesio-Lutherans found themselves, which are discussed in the following pages. For example, in 1572 the ministerium of the Swabian town of Memmingen issued a doctrinal standard to complete the town's rejection of the Augsburg Interim. Entitled "Bekannttnus vonn den furnemesten Articuln, Christennlicher Lehre . . . ," it apparently was used only briefly until the town adopted another confession composed by Jakob Andreae the following year. The 1572 confession is reprinted in Ernst Bizer, "Dokumente zur Geschichte der Confessio Virtembergica," *Blätter für württembergische Kirchengeschichte* 1951/1952:71–85. It should also be noted that the Philippist theologians of electoral Saxony did issue a confession when their sacramental teaching was under attack, *Confessio paucis articulis complectens summam doctrinae de vera praesentia Corporis & Sanguinis Christi in Coena domini . . .* (Wittenberg: Crato, 1574).

52. Chemnitz left this analysis in manuscript, and it was first published after his death, *De controversiis quibusdam, quae superiori tempore, circa quosdam Augustanae Confessionis Articulos, motae & agitatae sunt; Iudicium D. Martini Chemnitii,* ed. Polycarp Leyser (Wittenberg: Simon Groneburg, 1594), 2–5.

53. *Die Vnuerfelschete Augspurgische Confession Vnd Schmalcaldische Artickel, Sampt einer Vermanung Joachimi Magdeburgij an eine Ersame Landschaft Oesterreich* (Regensburg: Geissler, 1561). On the development of the *corpora doctrinae,* see Paul Tschackert, *Die Entstehung der lutherischen und der reformierten Kirchenlehre samt ihren innterprotestantischen Gegensätzen* (Göttingen: Vandenhoeck und Ruprecht, 1910), 592–610, and Wolf-Dieter Hauschild, "Corpus Doctrinae und Bekenntnisschriften. Zur Vorgeschichte des Konkordienbuches," in *Bekenntnis und Einheit der Kirche, Studien zum Konkordienbuch,* ed. Martin Brecht and Reinhard Schwarz (Stuttgart: Calwer, 1980), 235–52; and Gerhard Müller, "Das Kondordienbuch von 1580," *Zeitschrift für bayerische Kirchengeschichte* 49 (1980): 166–68.

54. *Bekentnis Vnterricht vnd vermanung/ der Pfarhern vnd Prediger/ der Christlichen Kirchen zu Magdeburgk* (Magdeburg: Lotther, 1550), A^v, [Giiij]^v–H^v. The confession was also issued simultaneously in Latin as *Confessio et apologia pastorum & reliquorum ministrorum Ecclesiae Magdeburgensis. Anno 1550. Idibus Aprilis* (Magdeburg: Lotther, 1550).

55. See n. 46.

56. . . . *solida & ex Verbo Dei sumpta Confutatio & condemnatio praecipuarum Corruptelarum . . .* (Jena: Rebart, 1559), also in German, *Confutationes . . . etlicher . . . zuwider . . . Gottes wort . . . Corruptelen . . .* (Jena: Rebart, 1559); see Robert Kolb, *Nikolaus von Amsdorf (1483–1565): Popular Polemics in the Preservation of Luther's Legacy* (Nieuwkoop: De Graaf, 1978), 202–06; and

Wilhelm Preger, *Matthias Flacius Illyricus,* 2 vols. (Erlangen, 1859, 1861; Hildesheim: Olms, 1964), II: 116–26, and 77–94 for details on events surrounding the composition of the *Book.*

57. *Bekendtnis der Prediger in der Graffschafft Mansfelt/ vnter den jungen Herren gesessen. Wider alle Secten/ Rotten/ vnd falsche Leren, wider Gottes wort/ die reine Lere Luthers seligen/ vnd der Augspurgischen Confession/ an etlichen oerten eingeschlichen/ mit notwendigen widerlegunge derselbigen* (Eisleben: Gaubisch, 1560), dated August 20, 1559.

58. *Erklerung aus Gottes Wort/ vnd kurtzer bericht/ der Herren Theologen/ Welchen sie der Erbarn Sechsischen Stedte Gesanten/ auff dem Tag zu Lueneburg/ im Julio des 61. Jars gehalten/ fuer nemlich auff drey Articel gethan haben* (Regensburg: Geissler, 1562).

59. *Der Prediger zu Bremen Bekantniss/ vom Nachtmal Jesu Christi. Vnd Doctoris Tilemani Heshusij Bekantniss vom Nachtmal Jesu Christi ...* (Magdeburg: Kirchener, 1561). The continuing controversy over the Lord's Supper elicited a confession from the cities of Lower Saxony a decade later, after Bremen had turned to a Reformed position: *Wiederholte Christliche Gemeine Confession vnd Erklerung: Wie in den Sechsischen Kirchen vermoege der Heiligen Schrifft/ vnd Augspurgischen Confession/ nach der alten Grundfest D. Lutheri/ wieder die Sacramentierer gelehret wird: Vom Abendmal des HERRN. Von der persoenlichen vereinigung der Goettlichen vnd Menschlichen Natur in Christo. Von seiner Himelfart/ vnd Sitzen zur Rechten Gottes. Jetzund Repetieret vnd Publiciert zum Bericht/ Warnung/ vnd Widerlegung/ von wegen etlicher newlich ausgepregten Buechern/ Darinn etliche newe Theologi zu Wittenberg der Sacramentierer Sprach/ Lehr/ Meinung/ vnd Grundfest in die Kirchen der Augspurgischen Confession/ vnter einem frembdem/ schein, sich zu vntersteben einzuschieben* (Jena, 1572). On the disputes related to both these confessions, see Theodor Mahlmann, *Das neue Dogma der lutherischen Christologie* (Gutersloh: Mohn, 1969).

60. *Confessio de sententia ministrorum verbi in comitatu Mansfeldensi, de dogmatis quorundam proximo triennio publice editis* (Eisleben: Gaubisch, 1565), issued in 1564.

61. *Christliche einfeltige bekendtnus der Euangelischen Prediger in Kernten/an die Hochloebliche Landstend daselbs vberantwort vnd verlesen im Landtag zu Clagenfurt/Anno/M.D.L. XVI.* (n.p., n.d.); and *Confessio. Christliche Bekentnis des Glaubens, etlicher Euangelischen Prediger in Oster-Reich* (Eisleben: Gaubisch, 1567). See *Confessiones ecclesiarum,* 35–52 and 53–113.

62. *Confessio ministrorum Jesu Christi, in ecclesia Antwerpiensi, quae Augustanae Confessioni adsentitur* (n.p., 1567). See Oliver K. Olson, "The Rise and Fall of the Antwerp Martinists," *Lutheran Quarterly* N.S. 1 (1987): 98–110.

63. *Confessionschrifft. Etlicher Predicanten in den Herrschafften Graitz/ Geraw/ Schonburg/ vnd anderer hernach vnterschriebenen: Zu Notwendigen Ablenung vieler ertichten Calumnien vnd Lesterungen/ vnd dagegen zu erklerung vnd befoerderung der Warheit, Zu foerderst aber wie ein jeder Christ die jetzt schwebenden schedlichen Corruptelen vnd Irthume/ nach dem Heiligen Catechismo Lutheri erkennen, Widerlegen vnd fliehen muege: Anno Domini 1567. Mense Martz* (Eisleben, 1567). See O. Meusel, "Die Reussische oder Reussisch-Schönburgische Konfession von 1567," *Beiträge zur sächsische Kirchengeschichte* 14 (1899): 149–87.

64. Magdeburg *Bekentnis*, A^v, Aij^r, Bij^r. The Austrian *Confessio* also, understandably, points back only to the Augustana, (Biij)^r.

65. *Confutatio*, (aiiij); Lüneburg *Erklerung*, Biiij^r; cf. the Reuss-Schönburg *Confessionschrifft*, Aiij^v, Dij^v.

66. Antwerp *Confessio*, (Avij)^r; Reuss-Schönburg *Confessionschrifft*, Aiij^v and Dij^v.

67. Ibid., Aiij^v; cf. Spangenberg, *Vrsachen*, (ciiij)^v. This theme was already present in the preface of the Magdeburg *Bekentnis*, Aij^v, Bij^r.

68. Ibid., Aiij^v; cf. A^v.

69. Antwerp *Confessio*, (Avij)^r; Reuss-Schönburg *Confessionschrifft*, Aiiij^r, cf. B^r.

70. Spangenberg, *Vrsachen*, Biij^v–Bv^v.

71. Magdeburg, *Bekentnis*, H2v–Nr.

72. Spangenberg, *Vrsachen*, (bviij)^r–c^v.

73. Reuss-Schönburg *Confessionschrifft*, Biiij^r–C^v.

74. Magdeburg *Bekentnis*, Aij^r, O^r. On the eschatological context of Lutheran thought in the period, see Robin Bruce Barnes, *Prophecy and Gnosis: Apocalypticism in the Wake of the Lutheran Reformation* (Stanford, CA: Stanford University Press, 1988).

75. Mansfeld *Bekendtnis*, Aij; Mansfeld *Confessio*, lr; cf., e.g., *Confutatio*, aij^v; Antwerp *Confessio*, Aij^r.

76. See particularly Gensichen, esp. 123–52.

77. Mansfeld *Bekendtnis*, (Avj)^v; Reuss-Schönburg *Confessionschrifft*, Dij^v.

78. Mansfeld *Confessio*, a2^r; cf. Austrian *Confessio*, Lij^r.

79. Antwerp *Confessio*, B^r.

80. Spangenberg, *Vrsachen*, A^r, (cviij)^r–d^r.

81. *Bekantnus/ des Wolgebornen vnnd Edlen Herrn/ Herrn Wolffen/ Herrn zu Glauchaw vnnd Waldenburgk/ ec. Fuer dem Churfuersten zu Sachsen. Darinn die Summa der widerwertigkeit/streit vnd vngnad zwischen Ihr Churfuerstlich Durchleuchtigkeit vnd jren gnaden stehet* (n.p., 1567).

82. Mansfeld *Bekendtnis*, Aiij^r–(Avj)^v.

83. E.g., *Confutatio*, Aiij^r and passim; Mansfeld *Bekendtnis*, (Avj)^v; Lüneburg *Erklerung*, Aij^v; Austrian *Confessio*, (Aiiij)^v; Antwerp *Confessio*, Aiij–Aiiij; Reuss-Schönburg *Confessionschrifft*, B.

84. Mansfeld *Bekendtnis*, (Avj)^v.

85. Austrian *Confessio*, Aij^r–B^v.

86. Reuss-Schönburg *Confessionschrift*, Fiij^v and thereafter.

87. Spangenberg, *Vrsachen*, aij^v.

88. Gospel: *Confutatio*, aij^v, Aij^v; truth: Mansfeld *Confessio*, a2^v, lr; Antwerp *Confessio*, Aij^v, Av^r.

89. E.g., Reuss-Schönburg *Confessionschrift*, Diij.

90. Bremen *Bekantniss*, Aiij^r.

91. Lüneburg *Erklerung*, Aij^v.

92. Mansfeld *Bekentnis*, Aij^r, Aiij^r; Reuss-Schönburg *Confessionschrift*, Ciij^v.

93. Lüneburg *Erklerung*, Biij^r.

94. Johann Wigand, *Historia de Augustana Confessione* (Königsburg: Daubmann, 1574), 13v–16v.
95. Magdeburg *Bekentnis,* Biij^v, (Biij)^r.
96. Mansfeld *Confessio,* a2^r; Magdeburg *Bekentnis,* Biij^v.
97. Ibid.
98. E.g., the Austrian *Confessio* labels its sections articles; cf. Magdeburg *Bekentnis,* Aij^v–Aiij^r.
99. Magdeburg *Bekentnis,* Biij^v.
100. Ibid., H^r, echoed in Mansfeld *Bekendtnis,* Aiij^r (Av)^r.
101. Spangenberg, *Vrsachen,* aiij; Mansfeld *Bekendtnis,* Aiiij^r; Austrian *Confessio,* Aij^v; Reuss-Schönburg, *Confessionschrift,* C^v–Ciij^v.
102. Ernst Koch, "Ökumenische Aspekte im Entstehungsprozess der Konkordienformel," in his *Aufbruch und Weg, Studien zur lutherischen Bekenntnisbildung im 16. Jahrhundert* (Berlin: Evangelische Verlagsanstalt, 1983), 34–47.

Index

173

Reflection Questions

Quite obviously, a grasp of the political, religious, economic, and social history of the 16th century is helpful for discussing Kolb's analysis of confessionalism. The Renaissance and Reformation Movements, *two volumes by Lewis W. Spitz (St. Louis: Concordia Publishing House, 1987), is one useful background reference for understanding the circumstances to which the questions refer. Because the following are reflection questions, specific answers to most of the questions will not be found in Kolb's book nor in other Reformation studies. The questions are significant for understanding religion, confessionalism, and present-day implications and applications.*

Chapter 1

1. Confessionalism is hardly a household word today. What impression does the term convey, particularly with the "ism" suffix?

2. Americans seem to react against the concept of confessionalism and the idea of having religious norms. Why is confessionalism seemingly not in vogue today? What evidence suggests that some other parts of the world may look upon confessionalism differently than Americans?

3. Our personal backgrounds are reflected as we communicate our religious views. How does our attitude toward confessionalism affect conversation about religion?

4. If the Augsburg Confession was so important and so basic, why was it so difficult to get agreement on the Formula of Concord in 1577 and the Book of Concord in 1580? What really made the Augsburg Confession of 1530 so important? Evaluate whether or not those reasons are still valid enough today to continue insisting on confessional subscription.

5. Why was Charles V anxious to squelch the Lutheran confessional movement, since neither the German princes nor any of the Lutheran leaders had really shown signs of disloyalty? What parallel political/religious situations can be cited today?

Chapter 2

1. What advantage or disadvantage comes with knowing the confessional stance of a person? How does that influence efforts to evangelize?

2. Was 16th-century confessionalism a lay movement, or was the laity (i.e., princes) involved primarily for the economic and political benefits? What is the evidence? Why did Luther and his co-workers involve political leaders? In view of later German history, was that wise?

3. Although all Lutherans subscribe to the same confessional statements, we may not assume that all Lutherans have the same theological understandings and outlook. What are some examples of differences? How can differences be reduced or eliminated?

4. Some hold that the differences between Luther and Melanchthon were substantive, others say that they were merely clashes over semantics. What were the stated differences? What might account for the fact that differences developed between Luther and Melanchthon? How could you justify Melanchthon's actions, and how could you account for Luther's position? Are there any modern counterparts or parallel differences today among Lutherans, or are they of a substantively different nature?

Chapter 3

1. We often look upon nations that are largely Islamic or Hindu as being very rigid and inflexible. Can you label them confessional? How does understanding such nations help us analyze ourselves? In the 16th century political leaders chose to assume direction for the confessional movement. Why? What else may have motivated them?

2. Luther and Lutherans claim that creeds and confessions are au-

thoritatively second to the Bible. What evidence shows that this is or is not true in practice?

3. Ecumenical councils in the early centuries of the church produced creeds that are still recited by Christians. With the advantage of historical hindsight that we have, how necessary was it really for 16th-century Lutherans to add to this base and formulate additional confessional statements? Who else at that time produced confessional statements? What was the function of such statements?

4. Occasionally Lutherans today call for new confessional statements. Other Lutherans have insisted that we cannot require subscription to additional statements. What are the arguments for either side? Evaluate the validity of those arguments.

5. On the basis of what Kolb has described concerning differences over adiaphora, how would you justify the position of those who refused to yield and those who were inclined to yield in this matter? What present-day examples could be cited where adiaphora are important? To what extent does doctrine enter into deciding for or against adiaphora?

6. Obviously, circumstances surrounding relations between church and government will change over decades and centuries. Nevertheless, the ever-present question for the church is, What is the proper relationship? How and how much should the church accommodate itself to government? What are some present-day church/government problems? How should the church go about responding to them?

7. On the basis of Matt. 16:24 Rabus characterizes Christian discipleship as requiring complete self-denial, willingness to accept whatever cross God "visits" upon the Christian, and steadfastness. What conditions today call for implementation of these principles, for Christians individually and for the church, in the United States and in other countries? How might persecution come today in subtle, almost unrecognized ways?

Chapter 4

1. Some denominations and religious leaders today have no concrete confessional statements. Since most Christians, like the Lu-

therans, base their religious beliefs on the Bible, why should any denomination develop confessional statements? How do such statements differ from Biblical teaching? Why do they differ?

2. How well do Lutherans today know the Book of Concord? How valid for today is the Book of Concord? Which confessional statements might not be acceptable to all Lutherans? Which specific statements within the confessions?

3. From our present-day point of view, the Religious Peace of Augsburg of 1555 provided for a strange arrangement, summarized in the Latin phrase *cuius regio, eius religio,* that the religious persuasion of a region's prince (whether Roman Catholic or Lutheran) determined the religion for all the people in that region. How could such an arrangement be justified? Are there any examples of a similar arrangement since the 16th century or evidences today of a return to it?

4. Kolb stresses several dimensions of confession—the act of confessing, the habit of confessing, and confessional documents, including official confessional position papers. What are examples of each? What are the uses of each? How might confessing become a "habit" today? What value might official confessional statements serve for legal purposes?

5. Political leaders played a major role in the emergence of 16th-century confessionalism. What difficulties would political leaders in the United States today encounter if they took a similar religious stand? How does that differ, if at all, from 19th-century United States?

Chapter 5

1. How do Luther, the confessions of the 16th century, and the Bible rank as authorities in the Lutheran Church? What difference, if any, is there between the stated rank and what happens in practice? How do other denominations respond to the concept of authority and levels of authority?

2. Confession in the 16th century, according to Kolb, was confrontational. Today confrontation would be considered inappropriate. Might that also have been a better way to confess for the 16th

century? What are the advantages and disadvantages of confrontation? What are the advantages and disadvantages today of packaging religious views in the most appealing form possible? Is it (always, usually) necessary to consider the wishes of others or even cater to them? How does the responsibility of the individual Christian enter into the question?

3. How specific must/ought one be in articulating religious beliefs? What should our attitude be towards other Christians who are not in agreement with our confessional statements? How do you distinguish between giving offense to fellow Christians (1) by not standing up for a true confessional position and (2) by being too firm and exclusive? What Scripture passages have been quoted in support of either position? How clearly do the passages speak to the situation today?

4. If, as all Christians seem to believe, there are clear Biblical principles and facts that ought to be accepted as truth, how, theologically speaking, can the contention and strife between denominations and individuals through the ages be explained?

5. What, in practical terms, does it mean to confess evangelically? To confess eschatologically?